The Road Ahead

The Road Ahead

The Automobile Club of Southern California

1900–2000

text by
KATHY TALLEY-JONES
and
LETITIA BURNS O'CONNOR

photo selection and layout by
DANA LEVY

PAGE 1: James Hansen's cover illustration for the May 1952 issue of *Westways* magazine, entitled *Spring Motoring,* conveys the romance of the road as a couple zips past rocky hills characteristic of Southern California in their MG convertible. Many of the original artworks commissioned for Auto Club publications, along with about 30,000 photographs generated in the course of various Club activities, are today archived in the landmark building at Figueroa and West Adams that has been the Los Angeles headquarters of the Automobile Club of Southern California since 1923.

Right: This neon sign incorporates the second logo of the Auto Club and the slogan Good Roads, which was a primary impetus to the organization in its inaugural phase. The Club earned the moniker Friend to all Motorists in the 1920s when its highway patrol offered emergency roadside assistance to member and nonmembers alike, an activity that won it wide appreciation from motorists and helped build its membership.

Contents

the state; and by 1925 Emergency Road Service was provided gratis to our members, a benefit of membership that still exists and is most often cited by new and renewing members as a reason for particiating in the Auto Club.

Motorists' needs have become increasingly complex: traffic congestion, aging infrastructure, and funding roads and highways today present challenges at a level we could not have imagined in 1900. The Auto Club continues to work on behalf of members to find solutions. We support alternative forms of transportation, including buses and light rail; our engineers are studying intelligent transportation systems, designing vehicles of the future to be guided by in-road sensors.

Just as Southern California has increased in population, complexity, and diversity, the Auto Club has changed as well. Our membership has grown to nearly five million. We still provide our core services of Roadside Assistance and maps, but the Club also offers full-service travel agencies and a wide array of insurance coverages. Today's busy members want convenient access to services. The Club has responded with automotive purchasing and loan programs, inaugurated a variety of financial services, and expanded office hours and telephone and Internet service. These contemporary efforts have succeeded because of the good work and determination of our staff and administration.

The Auto Club would not exist without the millions of members who give us their loyalty and employees whose mission it is to give those members world-class service. The stories of some legendary employees are in this book: the aptly named Dusty Rhodes and his equally imaginatively named partner, O.K. Parker, who traveled thousands of rough miles putting up road signs and making notes for maps; engineer Ernest East, who lobbied for roads that were well constructed; *Westways* editor Phil Hanna, who used the magazine to promote tourism while employing some of California's best writers and artists. These are the people who gave us our past, but our future depends on remaining relevant to our members and their needs. Today nearly 45 percent of Southern Californians are Auto Club members. That's a source of pride and a powerful responsibility that makes us look forward to the road ahead.

Thomas V. McKernan Jr.

Dear Valued Member:

The Auto Club has been serving members in Southern California for over 100 years and, while many other businesses and organizations have long since disappeared, we have remained strong because of loyal, long-term members like you. I want to thank you for your support of the Automobile Club of Southern California.

The Auto Club was created to provide valuable services to our members and all motorists. We posted the first road signs in Southern California and even some states beyond, all at the Club's expense. We offered maps and tour books, began providing low cost insurance in 1912 and created a roadside rescue service that evolved into today's California Highway Patrol. Our early focus on highway and transportation safety programs continues today.

From our original 10 members, we have grown to the nation's largest motor club, boasting over five million members strong today. To meet your changing needs we now offer over one hundred products and services. These include automotive services that range from approving auto repair shops to helping members buy or lease vehicles to teaching your children or grandchildren to drive. In addition to the AAA Triptiks® that we have long been famous for, the Club also has travel agencies in most of our offices and offers members a wide array of insurance and financial products. For over 100 years we have listened carefully to what our members expect from their Club, and we'll continue to work hard to make sure your membership provides great value to you.

Your role in this history cannot be understated. Your longstanding commitment has given the Club the opportunity to grow into the premiere service organization it is today. To thank you for your many years of membership, I am enclosing a copy of "The Road Ahead," a history of the Auto Club from 1900–2000. I hope you will find it both entertaining and informative, providing you insight into the history of your Club. We are particularly proud of the fact that most of the photographs and illustrations come from the archives we have maintained over the years. You may learn a lot about your Club that you didn't know before.

The Auto Club slogan is "We're Always With You." We're here today because members like you have always been with us. Thank you for your loyalty and happy reading!

Sincerely yours,

Thomas McKernan

Thomas McKernan
President & CEO

WE'RE ALWAYS WITH YOU.®

The Road Ahead

Highlights in Auto Club History

1900s

December 13, 1900—The Auto Club is founded by ten car enthusiasts in Los Angeles.

1903—The Auto Club begins to sponsor road races, rallies, and long-distance runs. In a time trial, Barney Oldfield breaks the national one-mile record.

1906—The Auto Club begins signposting. Within seven years, more than 4,000 directional signs are posted on 3,500 miles of roads.

1906—In adopting a broad public-service mission, the Auto Club lowers dues by 80 percent, from $5 to $1 per month.

1908—The Auto Club supports a bond issue of $3.5 million for better roads throughout L.A. County.

1909—The first guidebook, containing nearly 100 maps of roads and routes up the coast to San Francisco, is distributed.

1909—*Touring Topics*, the predecessor of Westways, begins publication. The first issue features the Los Angeles Automobile Show.

1910s

1910—The Auto Club adopts a resolution urging the L.A. City Council to ban stands selling peanuts and newspapers in order to alleviate downtown traffic congestion.

1911—The Auto Club's Touring Information Bureau issues its first maps over the counter, including one that shows automobile routes between the California missions.

1912—The Auto Club's affiliated Interinsurance Exchange issues its first automobile policy.

1913—The first Auto Club branch office opens in San Diego. Within the next two years, offices open in Pasadena, Long Beach, Santa Barbara, and Bakersfield.

1914—Signposting of the National Old Trails Route from L.A. to Kansas City begins. Today this historic roadway is better known as Route 66.

1914—Car theft reaches an epidemic level. The Auto Club opens a Theft Bureau that, in its first three years, helps recover 979 cars.

1915—The Auto Club begins participation in the Pasadena Tournament of Roses. For years, Auto Club tow trucks pull floats in the Rose Parade. The Auto Club enters its first decorated float in January 1994.

1920s

1921—The Auto Club establishes an Engineering Department to participate in broad-scale highway planning throughout the region.

1921—A Public Safety Department is formed to offer safety-education programs in schools, including the formation of a student Safety Patrol to supervise crosswalks.

1923—Auto Club attorneys draft the proposed California Vehicle Act, which establishes a uniform speed limit and other rules of the road.

1923—The Auto Club moves into its present headquarters at the corner of Adams Boulevard and Figueroa Street in Los Angeles.

1924—The Auto Club creates the Highway Patrol Service (later renamed Service Patrol). Roaming vehicles rescue stranded motorists, clean up broken glass, and offer first-aid, maps, and directions. By listing an emergency phone number in Touring Topics, on-call roadside assistance is launched.

1927—The Auto Club issues a National Parks highway map, which stimulates visitation to the parks.

1930s

1930—Auto Club engineers and cartographers mount an expedition to chart the proposed International Pacific Highway along the western coast of Mexico and Central America.

1934—*Touring Topics* changes its name to Westways to reflect a wider focus on Western living. Runner-up names include *Tides West* and *El Dorado*.

1934—The Auto Club holds its first Outing Show at headquarters; more than 66,000 people attend. The show displays the latest gear in recreational vehicles, camping, fishing, and other outdoor activities.

1937—Auto Club engineers propose a system of motorways to reduce traffic congestion.

1940s

1940—Arroyo Seco Parkway opens between Pasadena and L.A. Later named the Pasadena Freeway, it's the first link in the region's extensive freeway network.

1941–1944—The Auto Club joins the war effort. It creates special signs and maps for the military, participates in gas and rubber conservation efforts, and sponsors patriotic programs.

1950s

1956—The Auto Club purchases its first IBM 705 mainframe computer and revamps and centralizes all its data handling.

1956–1959—Due in part to a postwar population boom in the Southland, construction begins on 36 new or expanded branch offices.

1957—The Auto Club's Foreign and Domestic Travel Department opens; the cruise business is one of the busiest areas.

1957—For the first time in Auto Club history, annual dues are increased, from $12 to $15.

1960s

February 1962—A six-day storm generates 50,000 emergency road service calls from stranded motorists.

1963—The Auto Club works with the local office of the California Motor Vehicle Pollution Control Board to test emissions of 1,000 vehicles.

1967—The Automotive Research Center opens to administer testing of vehicle emissions and study air pollution control.

1968—The Auto Club launches BEBA (Bring 'Em Back Alive), a program aimed at reducing holiday traffic fatalities and injuries over Fourth of July and Labor Day weekends.

1970s

1970—The Approved Auto Repair Program is started to identify quality repair facilities.

1970—The modern TripTik is introduced.

1971—The L.A. Cultural Heritage Board declares the headquarters' Spanish Colonial Revival–style building a historic cultural monument.

1973—In response to the oil embargo, the Auto Club begins issuing a weekly Fuel Gauge Report informing motorists of gas prices and supply at Southland stations.

1974—Auto Club engineers serve on the statewide bicycle committee to promote bikes as an energy-efficient form of transportation and recreation.

1980s

1982—The Processing Center opens in Costa Mesa to house data systems and insurance operations.

1983—The Auto Club makes homeowners' insurance available to its members.

1984—During the Summer Olympics in L.A., the Auto Club helps organize pre-Olympic transportation seminars. Traffic flow during the games is the smoothest in recent history, thwarting predictions of gridlock.

1987—The Auto Club's alcohol-education program reaches 48 percent of elementary schools and 62 percent of junior high schools in Southern California.

1990s

1992—The Auto Club begins to offer AAA Visa cards to its members.

1996—The Auto Club's website is launched at www.aaa-calif.com.

1996—The Auto Club assumes responsiblity for AAA clubs in Texas, New Mexico, and Hawaii.

1997—The Processing Center in Costa Mesa is expanded and renamed the Administrative Offices.

1997—The Auto Club makes life insurance available to its members.

1997—The Auto Club–sponsored Graduated Driver License law passes in California. It requires teens to drive with certain restrictions (e.g., no driving alone between midnight and 5 a.m.) that gradually relax as the young drivers gain more experience.

1997—With sponsorship of the NASCAR Auto Club 200 at California Speedway, the Auto Club strengthens its role in motorsports events. The event is upgraded to the Auto Club 300 in 1999.

2000—Auto Club membership approaches 5 million. —Compiled by John Sherman and Leslie Mieko Yap.

The early motorist, attempting to navigate on unpaved, poorly marked roads, often had to resort to more primitive means of transportation to rescue his vehicle. When Auto Club Secretary Charles Hopper attempted to drive from Los Angeles to a tennis tournament in San Diego in 1909, his party had to be towed from muddy ruts four times before reaching their destination. Experiences like these spurred the Auto Club's campaign to develop Southern California's roadways as a means to realizing its economic potential.

"The most glorious climate, the most beautiful scenery of mountains, oceans, and desert to be found anywhere in the world. To open the gates of this paradise we need the key of good roads. Good roads mean development of the vast acres that are now almost inaccessible, mean the consequent enriching of the people and the state, and the progress of civilization advanced. This development work needs funds, and the Automobile Club needs new members in order to get the assistance necessary to carry on this gigantic undertaking. Join and Boost!" — "ATTENTION EVERYONE!" TOURING TOPICS, APRIL 1910

1
Good Roads

Introduction

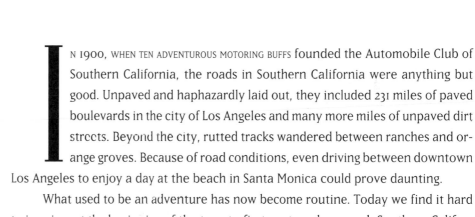

I N 1900, WHEN TEN ADVENTUROUS MOTORING BUFFS founded the Automobile Club of Southern California, the roads in Southern California were anything but good. Unpaved and haphazardly laid out, they included 231 miles of paved boulevards in the city of Los Angeles and many more miles of unpaved dirt streets. Beyond the city, rutted tracks wandered between ranches and orange groves. Because of road conditions, even driving between downtown Los Angeles to enjoy a day at the beach in Santa Monica could prove daunting.

What used to be an adventure has now become routine. Today we find it hard to imagine, at the beginning of the twenty-first century, how much Southern California drivers take for granted. Few people undertook today's long commutes between home and work at the start of the twentieth century. In 1900 most of Los Angeles's 100,000 residents lived close to work and not too far from friends and families. People got around by walking, riding horses and bicycles, and in horse-drawn wagons and buggies. More than four hundred miles of railways linked the area, including lines from downtown Los Angeles to Pasadena and Santa Monica.

When we hop on a freeway today, it's generally clear which way leads to Santa Monica and which to San Bernardino. Not so in 1900. No freeways had been built, of course, and wouldn't be for forty years. No organized program of road charting or signposting had commenced. The California State Highway Commission, formed in

The desert environment of the Southwest posed life-threatening obstacles to pioneering travelers like those stranded motorists in photos at right. By 1906 San Diego and San Bernardino counties had begun to mark desert watering places, according to G. P. Parmalee who worked in the Auto Club's signposting division for the first thirty years of his career.

This stretch of plank road, connecting El Centro, California, and Yuma, Arizona, was finished in 1916 by developers from San Diego. The wooden section of the road, six miles long and eight feet wide, incorporated 1.2 million board feet of lumber. It created a passable surface above the shifting sands, although keeping it from being buried required diligent maintenance. Double-wide turnouts were installed along the plank road from Holtville, CA to Yuma, AZ to allow broken-down cars to pull off and other vehicles to pass.

Taming the treacherous desert was one of the Auto Club's first successful lobbying efforts: it cooperated with and continued the signage campaign undertaken by the U.S. Geological Survey with federal funding in 1917.

1895, recognized the need for better route markers, but little had been undertaken by local authorities.

Few automobiles drove the city's streets in 1900, and a car bumping down an avenue might cause jeers, annoyance, or even fear. The first "horseless carriage" had ventured onto Los Angeles's roads only three years earlier in 1897. No manufacturer mass-produced automobiles—most motor vehicles in Los Angeles had either been built by tinkerers and enthusiasts or purchased by the wealthy from small manufacturers. Oldsmobile's low-priced, one-cylinder runabout did not hit the market until 1904, and Henry Ford's Model-T was still eight years away. Automobiles served as playthings, and very few people saw them as a practical means of transportation.

Primitive road conditions turned many outings into adventures—and automobiles themselves often proved erratic and unreliable. In 1900 automobiles looked like horse-drawn carriages and wagons—but without the horses. While they were sometimes luxurious, they were not enclosed, and drivers and passengers had to contend with being covered with liberal amounts of mud and dust. Drivers often started automobiles with a hand crank in front and fueled them with electricity or steam just as often as they did with gasoline. For example, Earle C. Anthony,

who later became a well-known auto dealer, built his own automobile by rigging a small electric half-horsepower motor to a wooden wagon.

The breakdown of a steam-powered automobile is credited with being one of the events that led to the founding of the Automobile Club of Southern California. As the story goes, a gentleman took his new toy out for a drive from downtown Los Angeles. Unfortunately, ten miles down Jefferson Boulevard, then deep into the countryside, the White's Steamer stopped dead. After trying to solve the problem himself, the driver sent for a repairman, who gave the car a quick once over, took a match from his pocket, and relit the pilot light. A happy solution—until the owner received a bill three days later for fifteen dollars, more than most workingmen would have earned in a week.

That day, the story continues, the owner of the White's Steamer assembled nine of his influential friends to found the Automobile Club of Southern California: William K. Cayenne, Lee Chamberlain, Arthur L. Hawes, Russell P. Holabird, William Lambert, Homer Laughlin, John H. Martindale, Edward T. Off, Harry Turner, and Walter D. Wise. (History has not recorded which of the group of ten was taken advantage of by the repairman.)

Although the mishap with the White's Steamer certainly makes a good story, the Los Angeles group typified the organizing efforts of early motorists in many communities across the country. Motor clubs had been formed in Europe and in several U.S.

When cars appeared on the scene, traffic in Los Angeles was already chaotic, with horse-drawn carriages, streetcars, bicycles, and pedestrians competing for right of way on the city streets. Motorists had to negotiate unmarked streets and confusing traffic laws that changed from one community to the next. Pedestrians were placed in perpetual peril by the mechanical monsters that had invaded their territory. The tracks of the streetcar system indicate the predominant mode of transportation in Los Angeles at this era, and as many bicycles as cars can be glimpsed in this scene at Sixth and Spring Street from the early years of the twentieth century, but the situation was to change rapidly as residents adopted the automobile as far more than the plaything of the rich, viewing it as a vehicle of personal freedom.

cities including New York, Philadelphia, and San Francisco. The move to found an automobile club in Southern California perhaps gained momentum when the National Good Roads Association held its convention in Los Angeles in October 1900. The National Good Roads Convention mainly promoted well-paved roads for bicyclists, but improved riding conditions for the two-wheelers also benefited automobiles.

In addition to the Good Roads Conference, a race held in October in Agricultural Park (in what is now Exposition Park, just south of the Auto Club's Figueroa Street Headquarters) demonstrated "the possibilities of making speed on the public highways," according to the *Los Angeles Times*. With automobiles so visible in the public eye, the time seemed right, and the ten motorists gathered on Halloween night in 1900 to launch the Club. Articles of Incorporation were filed with the state on December 13, 1900, and the Automobile Club of Southern California was born.

All automobile owners and enthusiasts within a fifteen-mile radius of Los Angeles became eligible to join the Club. An initiation fee of fifty dollars allowed motorists to join in addition to annual dues of twenty-four dollars; the first fifty members to join would be entitled to a 50 percent discount on their membership. At first, membership in the Auto Club remained the privilege of the well to do, partly because of the prohibitive costs of joining, but largely because ownership of the new and expensive contraptions continued out of reach for most Los Angeles residents.

Most motor clubs at the outset of the twentieth century were social organizations that sponsored jaunts to outlying areas, known as "runs," and races. In the early days, the Automobile Club of Southern California was no different. Although no doubt full of enthusiasm, the early members of the Auto Club took little action beyond organizing a few runs, and the Auto Club remained largely inactive for its first two years.

Believing firmly in the need for an active advocate for motorists, in 1903 a committee made up of Dr. Milbank Johnson, Fred W. Flint, Jr., Frank Garbutt, F. O. Johnson, and Harry C. Turner met to breathe new life into the Auto Club. These men had a vision of an organization that provided more than an opportunity to hold social events— they saw the need for an automobile club that truly provided much-needed services to its members.

Chief among members' concerns in the early years was that any legislation affecting automobiles be rational and not too restrictive—this included such matters as speed limits inside and outside cities. They also wanted more money allocated for the construction of good roads and improvement of highways, traffic ordinances to be made consistent between towns, and educational programs to be developed for motorists and pedestrians, including driver safety courses. The latter worried the general public—after an early fatal accident, the *Pasadena News* in 1905 noted "a large proportion of the automobile 'accidents' which have shocked this community and other communities are due...to the carelessness, incompetency, recklessness, or inebriety of the man at the controller and the character of his companions."

In addition to efforts to promote the rights of motorists and the education of the general public, the Club desired to promote Southern California itself. Most of the Auto Club's early members were businessmen aiming to propel Los Angeles toward becoming a grand metropolis—a mighty city with limitless potential powered by the automobile. Local leaders and Club members such as Henry Huntington envisioned monumental growth in the decades ahead. The Automobile Club of Southern California had positioned itself to be at the center of this expansion. After a few shaky years as a social club, it got down to real work.

By 1913 Southern Californians had adopted the automobile with a vengeance: there were more than twice as many cars per capita in the ten southern counties of California as in the northern regions of the state. Statistics like these were compiled by the Auto Club as ammunition in its campaign to allocate a "fair share" of state and federal funding for road construction to Southern California.

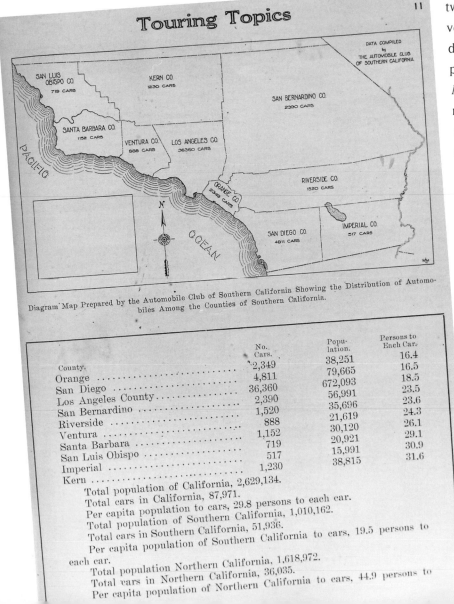

Diagram Map Prepared by the Automobile Club of Southern California Showing the Distribution of Automobiles Among the Counties of Southern California.

County.	No. Cars.	Population.	Persons to Each Car.
Orange	2,349	38,251	16.4
San Diego	4,811	79,665	16.5
Los Angeles County	36,360	672,093	18.5
San Bernardino	2,390	56,991	23.5
Riverside	1,520	35,696	23.6
Ventura	888	21,619	24.3
Santa Barbara	1,152	30,120	26.1
San Luis Obispo	719	20,921	29.1
Imperial	517	15,991	30.9
Kern	1,230	38,815	31.6

Total population of California, 2,629,134.
Total cars in California, 87,971.
Per capita population to cars, 29.8 persons to each car.
Total population of Southern California, 1,010,162.
Total cars in Southern California, 51,936.
Per capita population of Southern California to cars, 19.5 persons to each car.
Total population Northern California, 1,618,972.
Total cars in Northern California, 36,035.
Per capita population of Northern California to cars, 44.9 persons to

Officers and Directors

CHAS. B. HOPPER - SEC.-TREAS. ROY P. HILLMAN L. D. SALE C. H. HAMILTON

GEO. B. ELLIS - VICE PRES. G. ALLEN HANCOCK PRESIDENT A. F. ROSENHEIM

J. J. JENKINS GEO. PECKHAM

Automobile Club of Southern California

2

"Service to Members"

There is "a new life in the organization... making the Club more truly democratic and securing a larger membership so as to render the organization a real power for good to the motoring game."
—LOS ANGELES TIMES, 1906

1900–1920

The board of directors of the Auto Club included some of the most influential and far-sighted men in Southern California. Some are still well known, like G. Allen Hancock, who initiated the Club's signposting efforts when he served, 1907-1909, as president of the board pictured here; Hancock left his name on one of Los Angeles's loveliest neighborhoods. Fred L. Baker, who served as president from February 1911 to 1921, may no longer be a household name, but he was an important industrialist who served two terms on the city council, as well as sitting on the Board of Water Commissioners when the Owens Valley Aqueduct was being constructed. Other directors included Allen C. Balch, an engineer who founded the Pacific Light and Power Company; Joseph F. Sartori, who organized Security Bank; and Harry Chandler, publisher of the *Los Angeles Times*, who remained on the Auto Club's board until his death in 1944.

A MOTORIST WHO WANTED TO TAKE MORE THAN A SHORT SPIN in his new Stanley steamer or Oldsmobile faced daunting obstacles. Winter and spring rains choked roads with mud; summer heat layered them with dust. Even Vermont Avenue, a director of the Auto Club complained, "is worse than any river bed could possibly be." Deep potholes and ruts could snap an axle. Automobiles broke down—pilot lights went out on steamers, gas tanks ran dry, starter handles snapped. Each town and county set its own speed limits and made its own traffic rules, which unsuspecting motorists had no way of knowing. Promising roads turned out to be dead-end ranch routes and cattle trails. Insurance was barely an option—driving was too risky for coverage. Lawmakers did not understand the need for good roads; they did not grasp the vision of the automobile as a safe and efficient way of getting around.

To help solve some of these problems, in 1903 the newly invigorated Automobile Club of Southern California began creating its ambitious and innovative programs—it worked with the local and state governments to develop consistent automotive laws, raised money to build roads, and held demonstration runs to show the practicality of the automobile. Its promotion of service to members went hand in hand with the boosterism of the era, when businessmen were eager to promote sunny Southern

Because travel was so difficult in the first decades of the twentieth century, parts of the region that now seem to be in its very center were then remote, exotic destinations. "To the motorist who wishes a pleasant trip," advised *Touring Topics* in the April 1910 issue, "there can be no more delightful run than to go to Santa Monica and follow the coast road to Topanga Pass, over the Calabasas into Hollywood and return to Los Angeles."

This advice, which was augmented with a thorough description of the route, was timely because Automobile Club members had been invited to a "barbecue and bull-head dinner" on May Rindge's Malibu ranch. On April 23, 1910, 220 cars carrying more than 1,500 people assembled at Club headquarters in downtown Los Angeles and headed for the beach.

California to those who sought health, inexpensive housing, and fresh air. In the early days, business and civic leaders set the direction of the Auto Club. Abbott Kinney, developer of the community of Venice, was one such leader; Henry Edwards Huntington, who owned streetcar lines throughout the city, was another. A prominent physician, Dr. Milbank Johnson, was the Auto Club's first president. All these dynamic men infused the Auto Club with an adventuresome spirit and were well placed to raise the profile of cars and their drivers within the community.

As a start, the Auto Club sought legitimacy for its programs and its crowd-pleasing racing events and applied in 1903 to join the American Automobile Association (AAA), a confederation of regional automobile clubs founded the previous year. The national group approved the Club's membership, and it soon held a two-day racing event at Agricultural Park. "Devil Wagon Man Here Next Month," announced the *Los Angeles Times*, and everyone knew that meant Barney Oldfield, the greatest auto racer of the day. He set a national record of one mile in 55 seconds on the Agricultural Park track, and record crowds of paying spectators meant revenue for the Auto Club.

Club members also needed to convince local lawmakers that automobiles could play an important role in Los Angeles's growth and prosperity—and could be driven safely and sanely. The Auto Club invited members of the Los Angeles County Board of

From the mouth of Santa Monica Canyon—where an earlier generation of picnickers is shown with their horse-drawn wagons and posing on the rocks in corseted, ankle-length frocks in the photos at right—the caravan of motor vehicles proceeded single file up the narrow dirt track along the shoreline (left). The festive day featured copious amounts of food, prepared and eaten out-of-doors, popular music performed by a twelve-piece orchestra, and competitions including footraces, sack races, tire-rolling contests, and a baseball game. At the end of the party, the organizers toasted their hostess, the indomitable May Rindge who would later wage a battle royal with the state to prevent Highway 1 from traversing her land, but on that day she generously shared her piece of paradise with motoring enthusiasts.

The Panama-Pacific and Panama-Caifornia International Expositions, which were scheduled to open simultaneously in San Francisco and San Diego in 1915, offered a prime opportunity to introduce Southern California to wealthy and influential Americans from other parts of the nation. After securing the financial participation of the chambers of commerce and county supervisors along the route, the Auto Club undertook an ambitious program to signpost the southernmost of the transcontinental routes, the National Old Trails Road, which would direct travelers from the Midwest into the southern part of the state.

A three-man crew worked feverishly through the summer of 1914, planting "upwards of 2,500 signs," according to *Touring Topics* estimate, between Los Angeles and Kansas City. Their efforts bore fruit promptly: in the year before the signs were installed fewer than two hundred cars entered California over the National Old Trails Road; a six-fold increase was recorded in 1915, some of these 1,367 carloads of visitors undoubtedly lured by the expositions. By 1918 the National Old Trails Road had become a major thoroughfare to the West, with more than four thousand cars following it into California.

dropped its fees to a five-dollar entry fee and dues of one dollar per month —and by 1911 membership had grown to 3,200. The Auto Club also began new programs to increase its visibility to the motoring public within Southern California and beyond its boundaries.

Road Charting and Signposting Begin

Club members may have known how to find their way to Pomona and Santa Monica and Santa Barbara, but few in the general population did nor did they have access to such information. To help motorists find their way—and also to promote the scenery and sights of Southern California—the Auto Club began putting up road signs in 1906, an initiative formalized under G. Allen Hancock's presidency (1907 to 1909). "Our object," said secretary Fleming, "is to provide for the stranger, unacquainted with the roads. With the signs pointing the way anyone will be able to go touring with perfect assurance that they will not get lost." But before the signs could go up, Club directors had to decide just what the main roads were. They selected and charted routes to Santa Barbara and San Diego as well as Riverside, Santa Monica, and Redondo Beach.

When the Auto Club severed its relationship with the AAA in 1915—in part over that organization's demand that maps developed by the Southern California group be offered to other affiliated clubs—it added impetus for the Club to continue and expand its excellent and pioneering services in cartography. These editions were produced in a consistent style that reflects their era, between 1925 and 1931. The illustrated section of the Old Spanish Trail, circa 1930, which shows the route from San Antonio to Kerrville, combines precise descriptions of road surfaces, conditions, and mileage with flower-filled prose and poetic projections of Franciscan friars traveling this route in earlier times.

Kerrville, the next objective in the journey west over the Old Spanish Trail, is 68.5 miles from San Antonio. Leaving San Antonio, the route bears generally northwest, and traverses more or less rolling country the entire distance. Pavement is followed by way of Leon Springs to a point just north of Boerne, then graveled highway over slight grades to Comfort, along to Guadalupe River to Center Point, and to within 5.5 miles of Kerrville. This last portion of road into Kerrville consists of macadam, and is in excellent condition.

Masses of flowers meet the traveler's eye along the route, mingling their colors of yellow, white, blue and purple. Their perfume exhales on the morning air the same fragrance that cheered the hearts of the wandering Franciscan Priests as they plodded toward the Western sea. What feelings of thankfulness must have filled their breasts to view these radiant blossoms by hillside and hollow, their fresh and colorful beauty banishing for the moment the memory of the tangled gloom of the swamps and wilderness through which they had struggled in the earlier days of their journey.

Like the desert signposting campaign, the Auto Club's efforts to reverse the federal government's decision in 1907 to close Yosemite Valley to automobiles was orchestrated in *Touring Topics*. The Club protested to the Department of the Interior that leaving rail passengers seventy miles, or a full day's journey by horse-drawn carriage, from Yosemite did not permit appropriate access to this national treasure. Federal officials requested information about alternative routes into the park, and the Club dispatched a team headed by its chief engineer, O. K. Parker, to report.

The preferred route promised year-round access via a 32.5-mile road from Briceberg-El Portal to the valley floor, but the Auto Club was surprised when federal and state officials expected it to follow through on its lobbying efforts by financing and overseeing construction of this road. It rose to the challenge, selling five-dollar certificates to motorists to fund the roadbuilding project, which commenced in July 1913, after the ban on cars had been lifted.

The effort not only successfully developed tourism—31,546 visitors to Yosemite were counted in 1915, more than half of them arriving by automobile, compared with a total of 10,884 visitors in 1912, when cars were still barred from the park—it was a victory for the Club. "Scores of communications have been received," reported *Touring Topics*, "commending the Automobile Club of Southern California for its work in removing the Yosemite barriers that have so long deterred autoists from the enjoyment of the nation's great playground."

The profile of Half Dome (opposite) is as distinctive as the silhouette of a motor vehicle manufactured in the first decade of the twentieth century —and more enduring.

Auto Club Plans New Yosemite Route

The victory of the Automobile Club of Southern California in securing the opening of Yosemite Park to automobiles has resulted in a nation-wide recognition of the influence and power wielded by the organization and scores of communications have been received at Club headquarters commending the association for its work in removing the Yosemite barriers that have so long deterred autoists from the enjoyment of the nation's great play ground. It has been the impression of many automobilists that cars are already admitted to the park and this mis-apprehension has entailed a great volume of correspondence upon the Touring Information Department in correcting this impression. The Coulterville road has been officially declared open to autoists by the Secretary of the Interior but the date on which motor cars may begin the use of this highway has not been announced. The government has a force of road builders at work on that portion of the Coulterville road that lies within the limits of the park and it is expected that this work will be completed within the next few weeks, immediately after which it is hoped that automobiles will be permitted to traverse it.

A number of roads entering the park were inspected by the Club's engineer and detailed reports of these routes with estimates of the expense necessary to put them in safe condition were transmitted to the Department of Interior. After a careful study of the Club's findings the department decided upon ... route as the one most feasibl... tion and has gone ... early ...

leading to Yosemite and then completes the fina of his journey into the park itself. Great tree were ancient thousands of years before the ti Christ, rear their tops hundreds of feet in the a their huge bases are scores of feet in diameter, are great precipitous cliffs, almost sheer granite that rise in awful grandeur above the traveler views of distant mountains and sunkissed valleys flashing mountain streams and water falls that in t leap dwarf by hundreds of feet the falls of Niag There are shimmering pools in the fastnesses of park in which are reflected the towering minarets a cascades and mountain cliffs so clearly that the wo seems topsy-turvy and bordering these pools are flow flecked rims of verdure that like a great frame set off picture of sublime beauty. Through these scenes t motorist may ride for hours over mountain roads tha are like boulevards in a quiet that is broken only b the dalliance of the breeze with the ancient redwoo branches and through the ozone laden atmosphere tha is perfumed with a fragrance of wild azalea blossoms and pine needles.

With the opening of the Coulterville road motorists for a brief six or seven months will ... joy without restraint th... this wonderl... the ...

5

Club Plans to Finance Yosemite Road

The campaign of the Automobile Club of Southern California for a new roadway into Yosemite that will be open during the entire twelve months of the year and which will provide a highway of easy and safe grades for motor cars into California's greatest park, has now reached a point where the directors of the organization are able to announce authoritively that the proposed highway is entirely feasible and that the project will be pushed to completion within the next eighteen months. The preliminary survey of the route which enters the park from Merced by way of Mariposa and the Merced River valley was made several months ago by the chief engineer of the Automobile Club. From the reconnaissance made at that time it appeared that a highway could be constructed from Merced into the park that would have a total length of approximately sixty-five miles and which would avoid the six thousand and seven thousand feet altitudes of the other roads into the valley. Following the report of the Club's engineer a crew was dispatched to the Yosemite district and is now engaged in the actual final survey of the roadway, which will provide ... finished within a few weeks, and which will ...

... of the cost of the new

...ched to the state
...mobile Club it was
...tate and National
...se of constructing
...lub would lend the
...nent in an advisory
...however, were not
...ction of the highway
...ternative proposition
...as far as Mariposa,
...Automobile Club to
...to the Park with the
...d Federal authorities
...portion which is ap-
...ength. The reports of
...have indicated to the
...it is entirely practi-
...of thirty-two miles at
...orhood of $125,000 and
...o the motorists of the
...the Club has definitely
...m of raising funds for

...addressed itself to ...
the work.

The advantages of the proposed route over the present highways into the park are apparent to every motorist who has taken the Yosemite trip. The present roadways not only attain altitudes that render them extremely difficult to negotiate but they are dangerous many places and will always deter many car owners ... the Yosemite which is ...

to visitors for nearly half the year as the deep snows so effectually block the roadways in the summit of the mountains as to shut off all avenues of travel into and out of the park from October until May. The Club's road, instead of attaining an altitude of seven thousand feet, will be, in general, a gradual ascent from Merced to the Canyon floor and at no point will it exceed an altitude of three thousand feet. In addition it will have few grades of any consequence and none that will exceed five per cent and at a comparatively small cost it can be protected at all turns to make it one of the safest mountain roadways in the State.

The reports that the engineering department have made to the Club's directors show that there is no possibility of the road being closed to traffic during the winter months by reason of the snow for a longer period than two or three days. In case of an exceptionally heavy snow-fall in the mountains a temporary blockade of the roadway is possible but with the cessation of the storm the snow will quickly melt and all trace of it can be easily and rapidly removed. Further information as to the difficulties of constructing the road is required before it is possible to accurately estimate the cost of building or the length of time required to finish it, but it is known that practically half of the entire mileage presents no engineering difficulties, whatever as the roadway for that length will follow the valley and plateau land where no rockwork is required. The remaining distance of about fifteen miles is of mountainous character where the highway must be constructed along the sides of cliffs and it is upon this portion of the route that most of the time and money will need to be expended.

Until the final report is in and the Club's directors know the approximate total amount that must be raised to finance the building of that part of the highway to which the Club is pledged, no detailed plans for the raising of the fund will be announced. However, the tentative plan that the Club has in mind provides for a state-wide and perhaps a national campaign for funds among automobile owners and civic organizations. The importance of the project is so manifest and the benefits to the state as a whole and to individual motorists are so apparent that no difficulty is anticipated by the Club in securing the money within a very few weeks after the subscription lists are open, for it can be clearly seen that thousands of automobilists of the East will make the California trip in the winter if to the present touring advantages of the state during those months is added the opportunity to visit one of America's great natural play grounds in their cars, and this at a time when most of the other great parks of the country are closed to the tourists and shut off from the outside world.

The members of the Automobile Club who have given their attention to this ambitious road building project ... are unanimously enthusiastic over it ...

The Sentinel Hotel, Yosemite Valley, Cal.

VACATIONING
in Our
National Parks

OVERHANGING ROCK,
YOSEMITE VALLEY

Photographs by
WIEDERSEDER

FOR those who are planning their summer tour in the family chariot the National Park system of the West should make a real appeal. No better place could be found to make a short trip than one of these well conducted bits of public property and, if one has time, a tour covering half a dozen or more of them would be a splendid thing.

Improved roads leading to the western parks and monuments make them easy of access from all parts of the West and within the parks the government roads are well built and well kept making motoring a real pleasure.

The Touring Bureau of the Automobile Club of Southern California has compiled a brief resume of the western parks, their attractions and other necessary information regarding them which is presented herewith in brief form. Anyone planning a trip to any or all of the parks can secure more detailed information by communicating with the Touring Bureau.

Yellowstone National Park—Located in Northwestern Wyoming — 3,348 square miles in area. This park has entrances from all four sides; the roads from all entrances enter a central belt

road, which ___
through the ___
places of inter ___
are scattered ___
venient point ___
smaller camps ___
grounds for ___
may enter and ___
6 a. m. and 9: ___
entrances. Per ___
the ranger stat ___
bile enters—an ___
mite to use all ___
It is good for th ___
ing December 3 ___
The entrance f ___
$7.50.

Yosemite Nat ___
in middle easter ___
square miles 1,1 ___
roads leading int ___
west, all of whi ___
Joaquin Valley ___
Park boundaries.

The Tioga Roa ___

TOURING BUREAU
ROUTE AND MAD SERVICE
AUTOMOBILE CLUB OF SOUTHERN CALIFORNIA
1344 SO. FIGUEROA ST. LOS ANGELES

Map Showing Main Automobile Routes to
Lake Tahoe and California National Parks,
With Tioga Road and Connecting Highways.

SCALE · IN · MILES

AUTOMOBILE CLUB OF SOUTHERN CALIFORNIA
1344 SO FIGUEROA ST. LOS ANGELES

Buoyed by its success in Yosemite, the Auto Club undertook a similar and equally successful effort to construct an up-to-date roadway into Sequoia National Park. *Touring Topics* regularly published features on the parks, quoting at length descriptions by John Muir, Yosemite's poet laureate, in its July 1914 issue:

"Of this glorious range (the Sierra Nevada) the Yosemite National Park is the central section, thirty-six miles in length and forty-eight miles in breadth. The famous Yosemite Valley lies in the heart of it and it includes the headwaters of the Tuolumne and Merced Rivers, two of the most songful streams in the world, innumerable lakes and waterfalls and smooth silky lawns; the noblest forests; the loftiest granite domes; the deepest ice-sculptured canyons; the brightest crystalline pavements, and snowy mountains soaring into the sky, twelve and thirteen thousand feet, arranged in open ranks and spiry, pinnacled groups, partially separated by tremendous canyons and amphitheatres, gardens on their sunny brows, avalanches thundering down their long, white slopes, cataracts roaring, and foaming in the crooked, rugged gorges, and glaciers in their shadowy recesses working in silence, slowly contemplating their sculpture; new born lakes at their feet, blue and green, free or encumbered with drifting ice-bergs like miniature Arctic oceans, shining, sparkling, calm as stars."

Just in time for summer touring, the magazine revisited the national parks of the West in 1917, updating its reports on various access routes and publishing its own maps of them.

1918   TOURING TOPICS FOR JUNE   7

Club Inspects Roads of California National Parks
Highways of Federal Reserves and Sierra Points Covered in Two Thousand Mile Inspection Tour

THOSE cute little motor trips, suggested by the Automobile Club's Touring Information Bureau and published almost daily in the Southern California newspapers are all very well. They are enjoyable. They present a diversity of scenery. They even produce a pleasurable thrill in the heart of the motorist who hasn't had large opportunity to try out his car on long distance journeys.

But to the road men of the Club's Touring Bureau these are unimportant and insipid jaunts. For

Such a trip is a really big trip even for an Automobile Club scout. Such a one if taken about twice yearly.

Another tour—just an ordinary average tour—was completed late last month by still another member of the Touring Bureau's force. This trip totalled 2038 miles, occupied fourteen days' time and was made with the purpose to secure authentic, first-hand information on road conditions into California's national parks and other Sierra mountain vacation objectives. General Grant National Park,

Some of the Sierra Roadways Traversed by Club's Inspection Car

when these gentry tour, they tour. A trip for them means covering *some* territory.

At present one of the Club's professional "tourists" is somewhere in Kansas returning to this favored clime from a trip that will encompass six thousand miles of roadway and which will traverse a half dozen States. When this man gets back to Los Angeles you will be able to learn all about road conditions on the Midland Trail and he will be able to answer all further questions as to the state of the Lincoln Highway through Nevada, Utah, Colorado, Wyoming and Nebraska. Then, if you desire information on the National Old Trails road, he will have the very latest data for you, since that is the highway he is now covering on his way home.

Sequoia National Park and Yosemite—all were visited by the Club's scout, not to mention Kern River Canyon, Huntington Lake, the Pines and the Placerville-Lake Tahoe road to the last final, unbreakable snowdrift that was unsurmountable for the car and which turned it back when two miles from the summit and almost within sight of Lake Tahoe.

While the primary object of the trip was to procure information on the National Parks and Sierra highways, advantage was taken of the opportunity to cover both the Inland and Coast routes between Los Angeles and San Francisco in order that highway conditions could be reported and the Club's sign system be inspected.

The Club car left Los Angeles at six-thirty on

Signs and maps, emblazoned with the Club's distinctive wheel logo, served a dual purpose of aiding motorists and promoting the Auto Club. Hancock's legacy was continued and shaped by Standish Mitchell. Mitchell became secretary and chief administrator of the Auto Club in 1914, and continued to support the signposting program until he retired from the Auto Club forty-one years later in 1955.

The Auto Club released its first TourBook in 1909 to encourage tourism and provide information to the motoring public. This 388-page tome, which included nearly 100 maps of Southern California roads and lists of local traffic laws, noted that the Auto Club had spent $12,000 on some 1,400 road signs across the West. The road-charting team of O. K. Parker and "Dusty" Rhodes traveled nearly 1,500 miles of California roads to contribute information to the TourBook as well as to strip maps released by the Auto Club starting in 1912. The Touring Information Bureau had been established in 1911; members could call in person or by telephone to receive information on road conditions, including washed-out roads and those that were impossibly muddy.

"Car forwarding," or transporting private vehicles by rail, began in 1916 to enable members to spend their vacation time touring rather than getting to their destinations. It became an international service through a French affiliate, with foreign insurance and customs clearance included in the package price. Domestic forwarding declined as transcontinental routes were signed and became more viable options, anticipating the era when driving the open road would be seen as a worthy destination in itself.

Perhaps "Climbing the California Hills in a Pierce Arrow" was to an earlier generation what "Get your kicks on Route 66" would be in a later era. The Club's annual TourBook—the first edition appeared in 1909 and featured more than one hundred maps—was an essential reference for charting the motorist's route through California and beyond.

In 1910 the Auto Club hired a full-time sign maker to manufacture the distinctive blue and white enamel signs that dotted Los Angeles. Soon after, the Auto Club began its road-charting program. In 1913 it purchased a truck to chart roads, and in that year the Auto Club had covered 3,495 miles and placed 4,510 signs on routes from the Mississippi River to California. Why did the Auto Club go so far afield in its efforts? Signposting and road charting were valuable services to members, but they were also a way to attract and direct potential visitors and settlers to Southern California. Boosters expected expositions held in San Francisco and San Diego in 1915 to bring visitors to California; Auto Club directors wanted to ensure that as many as possible found their way to Los Angeles.

In 1914 the Club posted signs on the National Old Trails Route from Los Angeles to Kansas City. Also known as the Old Santa Fe Trail, the Club's cartographers chose the route because it generally followed the line of the Santa Fe Railway and had a good climate, scenic attractions and adequate hotel and garage accommodations, including the Harvey House hotels.

Climbing the California Hills in a 6-48 Pierce Arrow

, involves no more discomfort than riding in a Pullman.   This powerful touring car glides easily and quickly up grade and over mountain roads at an even pace.

W. E. BUSH, Exclusive Dealer in Pierce Arrow Cars

1227-29 So. Main St.   Los Angeles

Pierce Arrow Motor Car Company ──────────── Licensed under Selden Patent

Although car manufacturers had been banned from the Auto Club's board to keep its focus on member services, they supported Club goals by advertising in *Touring Topics*, along with competing map publishers.

The Auto Club's efforts in signposting major roads outside of Los Angeles County and its support for county bond issues that affected road building in those areas won it broad popular support and helped convince the competing independent motoring clubs to affiliate with the Automobile Club of Southern California. The Club spearheaded the campaign to construct a permanent coastal roadway connecting Los Angeles with Santa Barbara: the plank roadway (seen at right and at top right in the composite layout below) replaced a low-tide-only race up the beach and around Rincon Point; a permanent inland route was constructed about a decade later. As soon as passable roads were in place, the Auto Club used its magazine to encourage tourism, publishing articles that touted various aspects of the region as well as its signature routing maps. By 1915 motorists in Santa Barbara County had decided to ally themselves with the Automobile Club of Southern California, which opened its first district office in that community that year.

A Heritage From the Padres
The Magnificent County of Ventura, with its Beginning far Back in the Days of Spanish Occupation, is Today one of the Richest and Most Productive Sections of California

One of the Wooden Causeways on the Rincon Sea-Level Road

Attractions for Motorists in Santa Barbara County

Thatched Cottages on the Beach Boulevard.

Famous Motor Roads of Southern California

THESE ILLUSTRATIONS TESTIFY TO CALIFORNIA'S HIGHWAY ENTERPRISE.
With Nearly Ten Thousand Miles of Highly Improved Motor Roads in the State There Is Ample Opportunity for the Automobilist to Take His Pick of the Varied Scenic Routes That Traverse the Noted Touring Grounds of the Southern Part of California.

Tourism and *Touring Topics*

Auto Club directors and Southern California boosters believed tourism was one of the keys to promoting growth in the region. An early route through California charted for encouraging tourism and supported by the Auto Club was El Camino Real, "The King's Highway," which connected the Franciscan missions of California between San Diego and San Francisco. Club Secretary Fleming, also president of the El Camino Real Association, was the guiding light for the restoration and promotion of the route, which began in 1904. Replicas of a Franciscan mission bell, along with mileage and direction signs, were posted from San Diego to Paso Robles.

Even in the early part of the century, motorists found the Yosemite Valley to be a favorite destination, although the road there was challenging and tortuous. In 1907 the U.S. Department of the Interior closed Yosemite Valley to autos, and in 1911 the Auto Club began a fight to reopen it, a battle it won in 1913. In 1912, before the lifting of the auto ban, 10,884 visitors came to Yosemite. By 1915 31,546 poured into the park, more than half of them arriving by auto-

To provide some key to the history and identity of Southern California for settlers from other parts of the country, boosters turned to the mission era and found an icon that became a distinctive and dominant style for the region. The white-washed walls, red-tiled roofs, and arched colonnades suggested a historic civilization in this place that the raw landscape itself sometimes disguised.

A. P. Fleming served as both secretary of the Auto Club and president of the El Camino Real Association in 1904, when the effort to preserve the route linking the Franciscan missions was inaugurated. Replicas of the mission bell were installed along the route, noting mileage between each stage on the nearly four hundred miles from San Diego to Paso Robles. The Auto Club enthusiastically promoted El Camino Real, "the King's Highway," as the premier route through California, and its recommendation was quickly adopted by the motoring public. Charles Fletcher Lummis, who had served as the first city editor of the *Los Angeles Times* and as librarian in the young city's fledgling library system, had initiated its great western history collections, enthused: "No other state has such a rosary of architectural pearls of history, beaded along a string of 500 miles of such scenery."

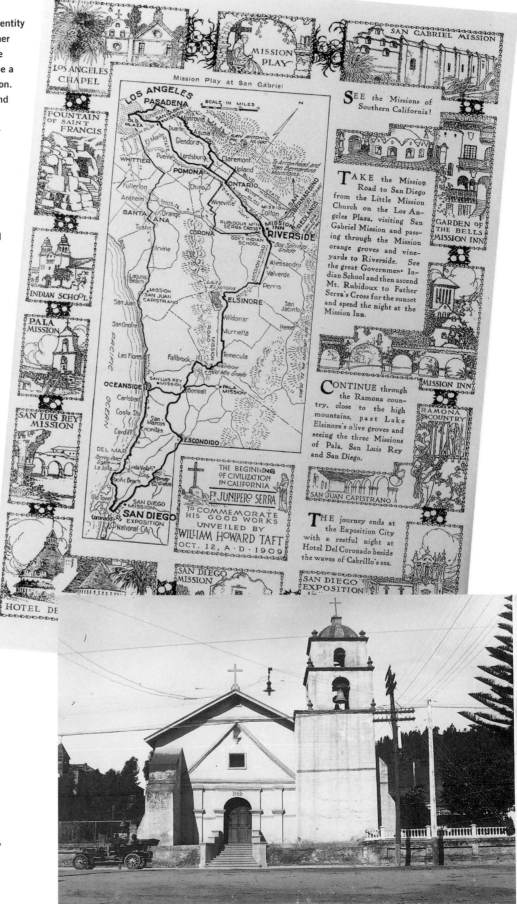

Mission San Buenaventura, located halfway between San Diego and Monterey, was established in 1782 as the ninth in the chain of California missions and the last to be dedicated by their founder, Father Junipero Serra.

Although the mission churches had been spaced at no more than a day's journey by foot to ensure safe passage for the Franciscan friars, in the motoring era visits to several of these historical centers could be combined with a hefty dose of scenery in one outing. Lummis, who had founded the Landmarks Club to preserve the missions and other structures of colonial California, was pleased to report in *Touring Topics* in August 1916, "The bewildering multiplication of automobiles and good roads has increased the visitation of the missions more than 10,000 fold within a decade. Whereas 100 strangers a month saw San Juan Capistrano, for instance, ten years ago, now 500 to 2,000 visit it daily."

A vintage sign pointing toward Mission San Fernando and Mission San Buenaventura was among those mounted in the first decades of the twentieth century to popularize El Camino Real, the first roadway—although it was traveled largely on foot—along California's coast.

mobile. The Auto Club then raised $20,000 by 1919 to construct roads that allowed year-round access to Yosemite Valley. The road, completed in 1926, created generations of supporters for California's—and the nation's—natural resources and parks.

The Auto Club also supported the building of some of the region's most scenic roads, including the Rincon Road to Santa Barbara, the Rim-of-the-World Drive through the San Bernardino Mountains, and the Angeles Crest Highway through the San Gabriel Mountains. Club engineer Ernest East monitored road building by public agencies and suggested improved techniques and new routes such as the Ridge Route Alternate, now known as the "Grapevine."

To further raise awareness of the region's scenic treasures, and to "create a greater demand for automobiles

Touring Topics

Although this Mission experienced considerable trouble with the Indians, it speedily acquired importance and wealth and in 1797 work was begun on the church, the ruins of which are preserved today. This church was built in the form of a Roman cross and was undoubtedly the finest of all the California Missions. It was built of quarried stone, with arched stone roofs and a lofty tower. The stone work was well carved and the ceilings were beautifully groined. The doorways were arched and in their carving and handiwork there is yet to be seen the high art of the master hand that produced them. This church was formally consecrated in 1807, with a pageantry of such gorgeousness and brilliancy that old chronicles contain marvelous accounts of its beauty and Indian legends relate its splendors.

This church originally had seven domes in addition to the great tower but a severe earthquake in 1812 shook down the tower which fell on the lower structure ruining two domes and killing a score of worshipers who were at their devotions. Later, about the year 1860, zealous but misguided friends exploded charges of gun powder under the structure with the expectation of building a newer and greater church on the site. The damage done was great and of the seven original domes but two remained. However, there is much here to interest the tourist and the unusually ambitious character of the architecture which these ruins show, indicates the magnificence of the original San Juan Capistrano Mission. It is estimated that it would require more than $100,000 to duplicate the church as it was at its completion in 1807.

In 1798 the San Luis Rey Mission was established near Oceanside. Although this Mission never attained the importance of San Juan or San Gabriel, it numbered its Indian converts by the thousands and the record of its achievements in proselyting among the aboriginal tribes is perhaps the proudest of all our Missions. San Luis Rey was founded by the Father Peyri. He became greatly beloved by the Indians and his co-workers and when, several years after he began his labors at San Luis, Father Peyri was called to Rome, it is recorded that the protests against his leaving were so vehement that he found it necessary to leave secretly by night for San Diego, at which place he took ship for the long journey to Italy. When it became known that he had departed from the Mission a band of five hundred of his Indian converts took their horses and started in pursuit. They arrived at San Diego just as the good Padre was embarking and two of their number swam out after the ship determined to accompany him. A boat was lowered to them and they were borne away with Father Peyri to the old

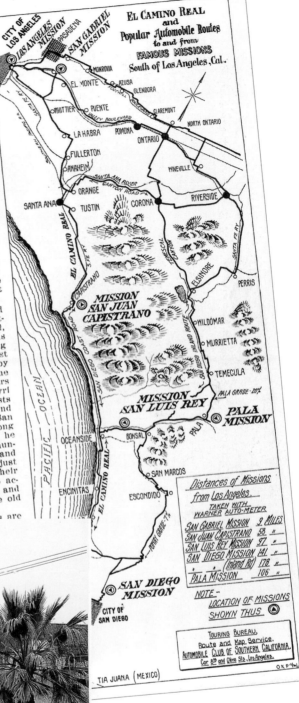

EL CAMINO REAL
and
Popular Automobile Routes
to and from
FAMOUS MISSIONS
South of Los Angeles, Cal.

CITY OF LOS ANGELES
LOS ANGELES MISSION
PASADENA
SAN GABRIEL MISSION
MONROVIA
AZUSA
EL MONTE
GLENDORA
WHITTIER
PUENTE
CLAREMONT
NORTH ONTARIO
LA HABRA
POMONA
ONTARIO
FULLERTON
MINEVILLE
ANAHEIM
SANTA ANA
ORANGE
TUSTIN
CORONA
RIVERSIDE
ELSINORE
PERRIS
CAPISTRANO
MISSION SAN JUAN CAPISTRANO
WILDOMAR
MURRIETTA
TEMECULA
PALA GRADE-20%
MISSION SAN LUIS REY
PALA MISSION
PALA
BONSAL
OCEANSIDE
SAN MARCOS
ENCINITAS
ESCONDIDO
PACIFIC OCEAN
EL CAMINO REAL
POINT GROVE-7%
SAN DIEGO MISSION
CITY OF SAN DIEGO
TIA JUANA (MEXICO)

Distances of Missions from Los Angeles	
TAKEN WITH WARNER AUTO-METER	
SAN GABRIEL MISSION	9 MILES
SAN JUAN CAPISTRANO	58 "
SAN LUIS REY MISSION	97 "
SAN DIEGO MISSION	141 "
(Inland Rd)	178 "
PALA MISSION	106 "

NOTE-
LOCATION OF MISSIONS SHOWN THUS ⊚

TOURING BUREAU,
Route and Map Service,
AUTOMOBILE CLUB OF SOUTHERN CALIFORNIA,
Cor. 8th and Olive Sts., Los Angeles.

The *campanario* (bell wall) with six huge bells—the lightest weighs 1,500 pounds—still stands at Mission San Gabriel Arcángel, the "Queen of the California Missions."

San Diego Run Sets New Attendance Record

IF THE Automobile Club of Southern California raises its collective hat and gives voice to one large and joyous "whoop," state authorities will have no need to ask the cause of the disturbance.

They will know that it is about the 1915 Motor Tour held by the club in question.

But the Automobile Club of Southern California does not "whoop,"—its triumphs come as a matter of course, and pass as they come, deliberately, surely and quietly.

If this organization cared to, it might point out

every opportunity to turn the gloom of the driving rain into the sunshine of happiness.

But the story of the tour is found more definitely in the final analysis of its results.

What did Southern California gain by the 1915 tour? It gained a reputation. There was scarcely a newspaper in America which did not, on the morning of April 24, carry an Associated Press or a United Press account of the excellent condition of Southern California roads which would permit of a continuous tour of one hundred and ninety-nine miles by two hundred and forty-seven automobiles

Club's Pilot Car Leading the Motor Cavalcade Into the Grounds of the Panama-California Exposition in San Diego. President Davidson of the Exposition and Secretary Mitchell of the Automobile Club in the Big Packard Headed a Line of Nearly Two Hundred Cars.

that the 1915 "run" was the largest ever held by any motoring organization, in point of the number of automobiles taking part, combined with the long distance—three hundred and fifty-one miles—covered. It might admit that there were no accidents recorded and that the two hundred and forty-seven cars moving toward San Diego and the Panama-California Exposition arrived, despite threatening weather and April showers, in splendid shape. Moreover, each occupant of those automobiles arrived cheerfully, enthusiastically and in some instances, damply. That perhaps was the greatest triumph of all—the great good spirit of those taking part, their willingness to overlook the minor difficulties, and their eagerness to grasp

in a single day. It gained a knowledge of the need for unstinted highway action—action, not on paper or in council chambers, but upon selves, over which crops can move over which visiting motorists ca gained more knowledge of the c supervisors of Riverside, San I counties with the motorists of S

Better roads are sure to follow ern California, at this writing, is most active territory in the wo building is concerned; although longer and better boulevards i nia than in any other part of Motor Tour of the Automobile

Runs, or road trips, had been one of the first activities of the Automobile Club of Southern California, but by the time this run from Los Angeles to the Panama-California Exposition in San Diego broke attendance records in 1915, the organization had developed the key functions and services that would make it an important force in the region's growth. Many of the out-of-state motorists who visited the San Diego exposition reached it via the National Old Trails Road, which the Club had signposted the previous year; by that date, drivers within the state relied on Club signage on more than 6,000 miles of roads in Southern California.

Despite this progress, many roads were still unpaved and either dusty or muddy, depending on the season. When touring in open vehicles like this Packard, which was the lead car on the run to the Panama-California Exposition in San Diego, motorists were well advised to outfit themselves with the gauntlets, goggles, and other "auto goods" advertised by the Hoegee Co. in an early issue of *Touring Topics*.

Where Direction Signs Are Badly Needed! A Roadway of the Lincoln Highway Signed by the Auto Club.

Club Cars Busy On Eastern and Local Sign Work

ACTIVITIES of the Charting and Signposting Department of the Automobile Club during the past few weeks include completion of the location of signs upon the Lincoln Highway between Salt Lake City and Omaha, sign revision and renewal on the National Old Trails Road between Kansas City, Missouri and La Junta, Colorado and similar work on the trans-Colorado connection between Big Springs, Nebraska and La Junta. This work is being done by the Clubs' transcontinental signposting crew which is now working westward toward Los Angeles over the National Old Trails route.

Still another signposting crew is now enroute to Needles, replacing signs and inspecting road conditions. From Needles this car will be driven to Parker, thence to Blythe, through [...] Valley, to Glamis, Niland, over [...] roads, thence to Campo, Descanso, [...] Mountains and return home by w[...] Lake, Pine Hills, Santa Ysabelle[...] Ramona and Wheelers Hot Springs[...] 2800 miles will be covered by th[...] again reaches Los Angeles headq[...] Club truck is covering the Dese[...] Victorville and Big Bear Lake re[...] way in advance of winter travel.

Here is Another Road in the Great West on Which Club Signs Have Been Placed.

Posting road signs became an important and visible function of the Club early on, one it would continue to perform for more than fifty years throughout the region and into other states. By signing roads of strategic importance, the Auto Club ensured that its logo greeted new immigrants who followed them West. These efforts were chronicled in *Touring Topics,* but the evidence was also to be found on intersections throughout Southern California.

by showing some of the pleasures of touring," the Auto Club began publishing its monthly magazine *Touring Topics* in 1909. Members liked it right from the start, and it soon had the largest circulation of any magazine devoted to motoring in the West. It kept members informed of every new signposting and road-charting project, discussed motoring etiquette, and alerted readers to legislative campaigns. Often, new strip maps appeared first in the pages of the magazine.

Touring Topics noted trends in motoring, including its observation in 1909 that there were only a small number of female automobile drivers:

"To be sure there are many women motorists in the country, and Los Angeles has some to be proud of, but of the large number of automobiles owned in Southern California, the number of women who are able to operate a car, without the presence of a sterner hand to guide them in case anything goes wrong, is comparatively small."

Touring Topics featured articles by such well-known writers as Charles Fletcher Lummis, who was the first City Editor of the *Los Angeles Times* and the first City

The Joshua tree, sentinel of the desert, supposedly received its name from Mormon pioneers who saw in its strange silhouette the prophet pointing their way. The flatbed trucks in these early photos are loaded with more precise directional and mileage signs. G. P. Parmalee, who joined the Auto Club's signposting division in 1923, reported "after three unsuccessful contracts with commercial firms, Club directors in 1909 decided to establish the Club's own sign crews. The first sign truck was a 1908 Maxwell, and the second a 1910 Franklin." In the annual report published in 1911, the Auto Club reported that $50,000 had been spent on warning and directional signs in Southern California.

Librarian. In 1916 he celebrated the history and beauty of California. The missions, he claimed, are

"among the chief material assets of the State,...the romance of their history, the picturesque beauty of them, the nobility of their architecture, attract more tourists to California than all its skyscrapers, gold, oil, or transit. Every tourist wants to see a mission....More automobiles visit them than visit the monuments of any other state of the union. No other state has such a rosary of architectural pearls of history, beaded along a string of 500 miles of such scenery."

Good Roads for Everyone

After 1910, with the introduction of the Ford Model T, automobiles became increasingly available. The development of good roads for all these new cars remained one of the Auto Club's key missions. The Club's directors hired engineers with national reputations to help give oversight to county road construction projects, which were sometimes more ambitious than local road builders could handle.

Until this time, Northern California held most of the state's population, wealth, and power. Many Southern Californians wanted more influence in the state legislature in Sacramento, especially on road building issues. The Auto Club did not hesitate

Auto Club signposting truck along a stretch of today's U.S. 25, which runs east-west between Santa Fe and another town in New Mexico, the lesser-known Las Vegas, both identified with mileage on the posted sign.

Joe Schaffer, near Pueblo, Colorado, with a Dodge Roadster and trailer, inspecting signage along the National Old Trails Route in May 1917.

Another member of the Club's signposting division kept a photo journal of his travels, which his son, Guy Duckworth, donated to the Club's archives in 1997.

A 1910 Franklin, like the vehicle that was among the first acquired for use by the signposting division, appears in this photo, but according to lettering on its side it served the Route and Map Survey Department.

The burros seem better suited to this landscape than the Auto Club's map and road-charting vehicle, circa 1912.

Signage pollution and vandalism had become serious—and expensive—problems. The Auto Club offered rewards for information on those who defaced signs and documented sites—like this roadside in the San Fernando Valley—where signs competing for motorists' attention had become an eyesore.

In its early years the Auto Club campaigned to allow motorists to determine the speed at which they could roll without endangering people or property, but without specifying speed limits except at intersections. By the time this sign was posted in Downey the Club's name suggested its approval of 20 miles per hour, which was the standard in residential districts. Speeds that are "reasonable and prudent" are still the basis of the current Vehicle Code, much like the standards the Club had suggested nearly a century ago.

to make its influence felt in the state capital and use the impact that its ever-growing membership could provide. In 1910 it opposed a state highway bond issue of $18 million because it didn't outline how the roads were to be built and because the state took over roads built by the counties without compensation.

Earlier, the Auto Club encouraged the legislature to approve the 1905 Vehicle Code, which standardized laws throughout California on such issues as vehicle registration, licensing, and speed limits. The Club also published a pamphlet informing motorists about the laws. Speed limits were a particular thorn in the side of Club members; a motorist driving through several communities encountered a crazy quilt of driving regulations: In Los Angeles, for example, the speed limit was 8 mph in tunnels, 12 mph downtown, and 20 mph elsewhere. Between 1910 and 1920, the Auto Club attempted to bring about a uniform vehicle code, work that would continue into the 1920s.

Expanding Services, Expanding Membership

Increasingly, the presence of the Auto Club was being felt beyond its Los Angeles home. Recruitment for members had spread outside of Los Angeles County and broadened to include other parts of Southern California when the Santa Barbara Auto Club

Construction of the principal north-south routes through California were financed with the state's first bond issue in 1909. In January 1928 the State of California adopted the federally numbered highway shields, but like this marker for U.S. 99, the signs still incorporated the abbreviation Auto Club So Cal. The recognition given to the major auto clubs that funded signage campaigns with membership dues, in the form of logo decals on the signs, angered other businesses, concerned by what they considered free advertising. A bill requiring the State Department of Public works to assume the signposting function passed both houses of the California legislature in 1933, but the governor, citing fund shortages in the lean years of the Depression, vetoed it.

In the early 1930s all existing road signs were evaluated and many were replaced to conform to national standards. The Auto Club agreed that the cost of the new signs should be borne by all motorists, not just those who supported these efforts with membership dues. Thereafter, city, county, and state agencies were charged the actual cost of materials for signage. Labor, equipment, and overhead costs of the installation were donated by the Auto Club until 1956.

The headquarters of the Auto Club moved in 1914 to offices at 1344 South Figueroa. More than 500 employees worked here in 1923 when they moved a few blocks to the new building at the corner of Figueroa Street and West Adams Boulevard that would be the Auto Club's headquarters and hub of its growing network of district offices.

1918

By 1918 a network of district offices had been established in the thirteen counties served by the Automobile Club of Southern California. The Club's presence in many different communities raised its prominence in the region as a whole and established that it was not only a Los Angeles organization but, as its name implied, the Automobile Club (for all) of Southern California. Many of the offices were designed in the Spanish Colonial Revival style, which recalled the Club's role in publicizing the restoration of El Camino Real, the earliest roadway in California, linking the Franciscan missions from San Diego to Sonoma.

A three-wheeled vehicle outside the Auto Club office at 758-760 Olive Street in downtown Los Angeles. This facility served as the headquarters from July 1911 to November 1914.

desire to publish national maps that the Auto Club had developed, and AAA's hesitation to sanction road races sponsored by the Auto Club. The Club dropped its affiliation with the AAA in March 1915 and remained independent for over thirty years.

Other important Club initiatives included the Theft Bureau, which began operating in 1915 and by 1918 had recovered 979 stolen cars. Also in 1918 it initiated free emergency road service twenty-four hours a day, towing automobiles that had broken down or been involved in accidents, making use of tow trucks it had purchased to bring in stolen cars that had been recovered by the Theft Bureau. Finally, in 1916 the Auto Club began offering a service to arrange shipment of automobiles by rail.

By the end of the decade, there were 30,320 Auto Club members. Southern California's population boomed—900,000 in 1910 and more than 1.5 million in 1920. In just twenty years the Automobile Club of Southern California had traveled far toward winning a place for the automobile in the regional economy, the political structure of the state, and in the imagination of tourists and residents.

The First Circular Board Track for Automobile Racing, in the World

A series of brilliant new racing records, an aggregation of the leading automobile "stars" of the day and the presence of the most prominent officials of the American Automobile Association rendered the Motordrome races held on the "piepan" track at Playa del Rey—the only track of its kind in the world used for automobile racing—of inestimable interest not only to automobile owners and promoters, but for the general public as well. The seven days of racing, with an epoch affording many a spectacular feature, marked an epoch in the sport. According to Association rules the contest was divided into three periods from April 8 to April 17 and from the initial performance when five national records were broken until the last memorable afternoon when Caleb Bragg, the young millionaire amateur, defeated Barney Oldfield, the racing king, for the second time, the events keyed enthusiastic crowds to the maximum pitch of excitement.

It was the first time that officials of the A. A. A. came personally to attend a race meet in the west. Chief among the eastern visitors was Samuel Butler, the "big chief" of the automobile world. As chairman of the Contest Board of the Association his was the final word on all matters passed up by Referee S. B. Stevens, who is a prominent figure in national automobile contests. A. L. McMurtry, chairman of the Technical Committee of the A. A. A. and the A. C. A., acted on the Technical Committee at the Motordrome and L. J. Wagner, well known as a racing authority, held the position as starter which he has assumed at many important eastern contests. The Motordrome track came in for its share of inspection soon after their arrival from the east, and under the ciceronage of Roy P. Hillman, Los Angeles associate

member of the A. A. A. Contest Board, and F. E. Moskovics, vice-president of the Motordrome Company, the newcomers looked on with avowed satisfaction at the practice runs that were going on. That the track would be sure to revolutionize automobile racing was the universal opinion.

According to official announcement events in which there were to be 250 entries were comprised in the seven days' racing card compiled by Walter Hempel, director of contests. Many of these possessed unusual interest aside from the reputations of their drivers, notably the big "Blitzen" Benz; the car which Barney Oldfield had sent by express at his own expense from Daytona, Florida. A fitting rival to this powerful machine was Ralph de Palma's "Mephistopheles" Fiat, the 200 horsepower car which was to have burned up the track against the Benz in the most sensational race of the meet. In addition to these two the world's records were ruthlessly smashed by such drivers as George Robertson, in the Simplex, one of the most sensational drivers in the country; Frank Lescault in the Palmer Singer, J. B. Marquis in the Isotta, Ben Kerscher in the Darracq and Caleb Bragg in the Fiat "90," the car which was given him upon his graduation from Yale only a short time ago and in which he startled the automobile world by winning out against Oldfield. The latter had three cars on the track, the Benz, the Knox and the Darracq. Al Livingstone of local fame drove the Corbin and Stoddard Dayton in several events, Frank Siefert the Dorris, Ray Harroun the Marmon, Nick Nickrent the Buick and Harris Hanshue the Apperson, which bore the distinction of being the only car in the meet to figure in a comparatively serious accident. Other cars

View of Motordrome Track with Grand Stand and Score Board

The Motordrome put Los Angeles on the motor sports map in 1910, when racing events began to be staged at the new venue near Playa del Rey. It was "the first circular board track for auto racing in the world," constructed of two-by-fours on edge, laid end to end to form a forty-five foot-wide track surface. *Touring Topics* (May 1910) described the venue enthusiastically as a "piepan," referring to continuous banking of twenty degrees that raised the outer edge twenty-five feet above the ground. This surface minimized dust, which plagued drivers and obscured spectators' views of races.

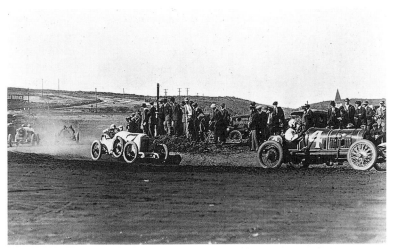

In this 1915 road race in San Diego, Eddie Rickenbacker—who won fame and the Medal of Honor for his role as a fighter pilot in World War I and went on to become president of Eastern Airlines —drives a Peugeot emblazoned with the number 7 at the center of the photo.

Racetrack in Agricultural Park (now Exposition Park) at which the Auto Club sponsored races in 1903 and 1904.

This view of Henry Ford Avenue in Wilmington shows the confluence of automobiles and oil wells that had transformed the Southern California landscape since oil was discovered in the 1920s. The auto industry produced nearly two million new cars in 1920, and more and more residents of metropolitan Los Angeles acquired automobiles and began to rely on them to get to work and for their daily routines. Membership in the Automobile Club of Southern California stood at 30,320 at the beginning of the decade, but by 1928 it had reached 129,536.

When the armistice of November 11, 1918 brought to a close the hostilities of World War I, the Auto Club acted promptly to get road building back on track, requesting that the California legislature transfer $3 million from the general fund to be designated specifically for highway construction. Preference in hiring for all jobs so created was given to returning servicemen.

3

"Model City of the Future"

1920s and 1930s

"The history of road construction in Southern California will read in days to come like a romance....The [roads] combine what might at first seem as unblendable as oil and water, the two extremes of luxury and necessity. The ponderous trucks of commerce, the richly appointed limousines of the wealthy, the touring cars of the visitors, the motorcycles of individual travelers—all... pass and re-pass on these winding ribbons of lawn-like smoothness.... Every highway is mapped and sign-boarded with the strictest care and accuracy by the Automobile Club of Southern California."

TOURING TOPICS, JULY 1920

AFTER THE END OF WORLD WAR I, the Club's service and leadership on the home front during the war had given membership a boost and generated tremendous goodwill within the community. The Club and its staff had made large purchases of Liberty Bonds and encouraged members to buy them through articles in *Touring Topics*. The Auto Club had also made use of its unique expertise—it facilitated the efforts of Army recruiters sent to Los Angeles to staff the ambulance corps and helped train the drivers.

By the beginning of the 1920s the automobile had become a fixture in American life, and the number of cars in Los Angeles had increased exponentially. A modest Ford Model-T runabout could be purchased for $290 (still a lot of money when the average weekly wage in Southern California was twenty dollars). Gasoline powered most cars, but there were still Coates, Doble, and Stanley steamers puffing around town.

In the early 1920s the economy in Southern California blossomed—people relocated in large numbers, seeking work in the oil fields in Huntington Beach, Long Beach, Santa Fe Springs, and the San Joaquin Valley. The movie industry had become the largest employer in Los Angeles by 1920, luring thousands to try their luck at becoming the next big star; often these adventurous souls became members of the Auto Club. *Touring Topics* seized upon the fascination with movie stars, running a piece in 1920 about actors and celebrities who were Club members, including Mary

Regular rivers, with water in 'em, in West Virginia.

May 24th found the traveling twins reunited at Albuquerque and once more started on their round trip across the country. This time they headed north over the dirt roads of the North and South Highway which connects the Lincoln and National Old Trails transcontinental routes by way of Colorado. A powerful day's running took them over 277 miles of the good dirt roads of this region with a night's stop at Trinidad. The only stretch that was not easy going was the mud flats around Wagon Mound and Springer and this was found to be greatly improved over its previous condition.

Another stretch from Trinidad to Denver, 248 miles of splendid gravel roads, was covered on May 25th and this brought a temporary halt to the trip while the travelers made up their report on road signs, road conditions and other features which were necessary for the log of the trip and the complete set of strip maps which will be forthcoming.

Three days of rest put the tourists in fine shape and they ripped off a record day's run on May 29th, covering a triangular section of the North and South Highway and the National Old Trails. Starting out from Denver in the early morning the car rolled into La Junta, back along the road to Trinidad and then to La Junta once more, a total of 359 miles, all along excellent gravel roads which made the big mileage seem easy.

May 30th took the scout car from La Junta to Kinsley, Kansas, a 265 mile jaunt along roads mostly in fair condition which as a general rule followed the section lines of the region. Between Oferle and Spearville the roads were very badly cut up due to their use by automobiles while still wet from the recent rains.

The last day of May was spent entirely in the state of Kansas, the club car traveling from Kinsley to McPherson and then making a side trip from McPherson to Lindsborg and Herrington and return to McPherson, the side trip being over a road which may possibly be added to the National Old Trails highway in the future.

The first day of June was one that Rhodes and Lewis will not forget for a long time. They pulled out of McPherson early in the mornng and set sail eastward with full speed ahead. They hoped to keep in front of a rainstorm which they had spotted coming out of the west but one of those rapid Kansas breezes blew the storm up on them faster than their eight cylinders could push them along and after bucking mud for several sticky miles they stopped off at Admire, Kansas, a metropolis of the great western plains where the entire population, all three of 'em, helped stow the car away in a barn. The mileage for the day was 116 and some of them were very long miles.

The remaining miles between Admire and Kansas City were covered through good old gumbo mud on June 2nd and there the travelers laid over for a week to complete their notes on the trip and get the mass of information in shape for use later.

The second leg of the eastward journey was taken up on June 10th with a 262 mile run from Kansas City to Wright City, Missouri. The roads were found to be in splendid shape most of the way, a four mile stretch near Mineola being the chief exception. The 30 miles immediately east of Kansas City were a boulevard and from that point on good dirt, gravel and rock roads led to the point where the Missouri River is crossed by ferry at Booneville. That barge is a great convenience and operates between 7 a. m. and 8:30 p. m. The charge is $1.08 per trip.

The brief hop from Wright City to St. Louis, 84 miles, was covered on June 11th and on June 12th the encounter

Ollie Lewis and one of the Automobile Club of Southern California signs on the Lincoln Highway shot up by someone with better aim than judgment.

"Signposting methods in the East and Middle West are certainly not up to the standard of the Pacific Coast," opined the unidentified author of an article in the August 1920 issue of *Touring Topics* reporting on the 8,881-miles coast-to-coast journey just completed by Dusty Rhodes and Ollie Lewis to prepare strip maps of the major transcontinental routes. "Ouija boards would come in mighty handy when trying to get in and out of many Eastern cities."

Vandalism had become a problem almost as soon as signs were installed; within a few years of inaugurating the program, the Auto Club was offering a bounty for information on those who defaced the signs. The caption on this photo of Ollie Lewis offers a dry summation of the problem: "sign on the Lincoln Highway shot up by someone with better aim than judgment."

Pickford, Douglas Fairbanks, and Jack Dempsey: "In this rapid evolution of the picture profession," noted an article in *Touring Topics,* "no one factor has had a greater influence than the automobile, and its accompanying adjunct of Good Roads. Scores of thrilling screen stories have used and are using the automobile as the main accessory for speedy and exciting action."

1923: A Watershed Year

It was an expansive time for Southern California and the Auto Club. In 1923 the state registered its millionth motor vehicle, and in May the Department of Motor Vehicles gave license number 1,000,000 to the Auto Club's Touring Bureau manager, Donald Doig. Club membership had tripled in three years, nearly reaching 100,000 in 1923. The Club employed 275 staff members in 1920 and increased staff to more than one thousand in 1925.

In 1923 the Auto Club built its new headquarters building to house its growing staff and serve as a focal point for members. Located at the corner of Adams Boule-

1923 was a watershed year for California motorists: the millionth car was registered in the state, and the population of Los Angeles itself had nearly doubled since 1920 to just under one million. Local booster organizations devised a new strategy to grow the local economy and fuel its population boom: the All-Year Club, which touted Southern California as a year-round tourist destination.

Harry Chandler, who sat on the boards of both the Auto Club and the All-Year Club, championed an advertising campaign in 1923 in the *Saturday Evening Post*, which the Auto Club supported, that targeted not the wealthy Easterners who already flocked to the region's mild climate in the winter, but Westerners who could extend the tourism season by driving to its beaches while the kids were on school holiday. "Come this summer!" trumpets the ad. "The world's largest Automobile Club invites you to Southern California, 'The Heart of Motorland' where scenic grandeur, 4,000 miles of perfect roads, and the balmy rainless days and cool nights of a famous summer playground make a motoring paradise par excellence."

vard and Figueroa Street, the building was designed by the architectural firm of Sumner Hunt and Silas Burns, its architecture echoing the historic missions the Auto Club had promoted as tourist destinations. Club directors had chosen its location wisely: Figueroa Boulevard was the setting of the popular comic strip "Gasoline Alley" and was lined with auto dealerships and repair shops. The building's inviting spaces helped members feel as if they truly belonged to a club when they walked in to pick up maps, buy insurance, or renew their car's registration.

Not only did members have the new headquarters as a resource for their motoring needs, but the Club had also expanded the number of its district offices—twenty-one in 1923, and another thirteen added by the end of the decade, all designed in the Spanish Colonial style that had become the Auto Club's signature. The number of district offices provides just one indication of the enormous growth that both the region and the Auto Club were experiencing. Under the leadership of Field Secretary Carl E. McStay, these offices proved that it was truly the Automobile Club of Southern California and not a Los Angeles club with branch offices in the suburbs. More than half of new memberships and insurance policies originated through the district offices at the beginning of the decade, and that rate climbed to nearly 70 percent by the end. Members took advantage of the services the Auto Club offered in record num-

Sumner Hunt and Silas Burns, who helped popularize the Spanish Colonial and Mission Revival styles of architecture, designed the Club's new headquarters which was completed in 1923. The building, an elegant structure with an octagonal tower, looms over the intersection of Figueroa Street and Adams Boulevard just south of downtown Los Angeles. Two-story arched windows on the exterior recall the covered walkways that enclosed mission gardens and themselves define a welcoming interior courtyard where such popular events as the Outing Shows were held.

Huge letters on the building's roof marked the location of the Auto Club for pioneering aviators, who flocked to Southern California's skies when the fledgling aerospace industry flourished in the region. A landmark church in the more baroque Spanish revival style called Churrigueresque, designed by Albert C. Martin and constructed in 1925, still stands on the opposite corner of the West Adams-Figueroa intersection.

Douglas Fairbanks and Mary Pickford participated in 1926 in opening the road through Laguna Beach that would later be known as Pacific Coast Highway. Hollywood stars not only personified Southern California's glamorous lifestyle, they drove its most opulent cars. The film industry already had become one of the region's major employers and attracted many new immigrants.

bers. In 1923 the Touring Bureau answered nearly 455,000 telephone calls and responded to 790,000 questions from members and travelers who walked into headquarters and the district offices. That year, the bureau issued more than seven million maps.

Charting and mapmaking continued at a furious pace. The Club created more than two hundred new maps of the United States in 1923 alone. Ollie Lewis and "Dusty" Rhodes continued their work charting the National Old Trails route, including roads to Washington and New York. Armed with a speedometer, compass, grade meter, and altimeter, the two men surveyed routes through the southern states that covered nearly 16,000 miles. Other cartographers surveyed routes in the north—and all their activities, including weather reports, strandings, and broken axles were reported in *Touring Topics.* The maps provided an invaluable service to members interested in trekking far afield. Tourists and would-be settlers also made use of the maps, pouring into Southern California, like "a swarm of invading locusts" in "rattletrap automobiles, their fenders tied with strings, and curtains flapping in the breeze," observed one *Touring Topics* writer.

G. P. Parmalee, who joined the signposting department in 1923 and worked there until the Auto Club ceased posting signs in 1956, noted that by the early 1920s, California, Nevada, and Arizona roads were well marked with warning and directional signs.

The Club expanded its network of district offices in the 1920s, along with the membership roles and territory served by the Automobile Club of Southern California. Because it was structured as a "club," members were expected to participate by coming in to the offices to pick up free maps and request other information. But the Club also needed to serve members where they lived; to make the public feel welcome, homey touches like fireplaces were installed in many offices.

The district office (top) opened in Taft in 1927; the fifteen-person staff of the Glendale office (center), 1930; this office in Porterville (bottom) served that region from 1920 to 1928.

An office in Huntington Park (top) was staffed from 1923 to 1928, but motorists in the San Gabriel Valley may have found the location at 332 West Colorado Boulevard in Pasadena (bottom right) more convenient: it operated from 1924 to 1938. A two-person office in the town of Bishop opened in July 1921 to serve Inyo and Mono Counties, the northernmost part of the region served by the Automobile Club of Southern California.

City streets were not always so well marked. The Club's first stop signs were placed in the city of Coronado in February 1925 and read "BOULE-VARD STOP" in red letters on a white background. In 1929 and 1930 all traffic signs were changed to conform to national standards for colors and designs for signage.

Traffic Planning Begins

All those cars and people had to go somewhere, and residents started to feel the downside to the area's growth. In 1920, 22,000 cars a day entered and left the city—even though this is fewer than might pass through the intersection of Sepulveda and Wilshire during a busy hour today, for a city largely without stop lights and traffic signs, this volume caused problems that produced increasing chaos.

The Auto Club pioneered the search for solutions to the city's increasingly chaotic traffic. In 1922 it commissioned and published a study that offered recommendations to improve traffic flow, including building more and wider streets, one-way streets in some areas, and crosswalks that limited pedestrians to areas

Broken glass posed more of a threat when inflatable tires filled with rubber inner tubes were the norm. The Highway Patrol vehicles launched by the Auto Club not only assisted vehicles disabled by flat tires but attempted to reduce the number of such incidents by sweeping up broken glass and eliminating other hazards to the motorist.

Official Garages and State-wide Emergency Service

for Members of the Automobile Club of Southern California and the California State Automobile Association

The Garages listed below have contracted with the AUTOMOBILE CLUB of SOUTHERN CALIFORNIA to give the members prompt, courteous and efficient service at reasonable prices.

Members are advised to patronize these establishments. Any discourtesy or inattention should be immediately reported to the Secretary. It is suggested that members show their cards.

How to Obtain Free Emergency Service

Official Stations for Emergency Road Service in Southern California are designated by star and phone number

STATEWIDE EMERGENCY SERVICE is furnished to members through competent garages designated as Official Emergency Service Stations of the Automobile Club of Southern California and the California State Automobile Association.

¶ Members are entitled to free emergency service only when service is rendered by official service stations. In Northern and Central California by the service stations of the California State Automobile Association, and in Southern California by the service stations of the Automobile Club of Southern California.

¶ The nearest official station is to be called.

¶ The object of Emergency Service, is to assist in an emergency the member whose car has become disabled, the service man who answers the call will either start your car in 30 minutes' mechanical labor or tow it to the protection of the Emergency Service Station called.

¶ Towing elsewhere at member's expense.

¶ This service is for emergencies when car is disabled, and does not apply on mechanical or repair work at garages, nor include supplies or parts.

¶ Tire service—changing spare tire from rack to rim—will be extended to members but does not include the repair to tires or tubes.

¶ Carry the current issue of the Club magazine, TOURING TOPICS, containing list of appointed garages, in your car.

HOW TO OBTAIN SERVICE

¶ Members with their disabled cars outside of Los Angeles are requested to call the nearest Emergency Service Station—listed in each issue of TOURING TOPICS or this booklet. In or near Los Angeles City, call Club headquarters, Richmond 3111—always [...]

¶ When car develops trouble at any location where it is not practical or possible to tow it out with nearest available equipment, and it is necessary to return to the service station for additional equipment or for parts to repair car at location, the Club will assume cost of one round trip and thirty minutes labor at car, and members will be required to pay for additional time and trips.

¶ This is strictly an emergency service for members only whose cars are disabled. This service is not available for cars at or in public garages, when intentionally driven off public highways into vacant lots, open fields, creek beds, beaches, hunting grounds, etc.

¶ When unusual conditions exist, such as slides, washed-out roads, etc., where there is little chance of a car getting through without trouble, the Club will not assume the cost if the member requires emergency service.

¶ Service can not apply when a member is riding in car of a non-member and owner of car is present.

¶ Free service is restricted to passenger cars and does not include trucks, delivery cars, buses, motorcycles or any motor vehicle equipped with a commercial, camp or delivery body.

¶ Payment of tow bills incurred by members with garages which are not duly appointed official Emergency Service Stations of the Automobile Club of Southern California or the California State Automobile Association.

¶ Members cannot be reimbursed for any service incurred through failure of messenger to deliver above information to the proper official station.

¶ Service cannot apply to employes or friends of members who do not belong, even when such employes or friends are operating the member's cars, as Club service follows the member and not the car.

¶ Garages are instructed to collect for towing, or service, when member does not have a paid-up membership card.

¶ Service for any truck, bus or trailer.

¶ Service for any car is disabled when it is located outside [...] service when a car is disabled [...] Official Emergency Service

The Auto Club's Highway Patrol, which predated the California Highway Patrol, offered service to stranded motorists whether they were Auto Club members or not, earning it the moniker "Good Samaritans of the Highway" and much good will for the Club. The fleet of eleven light trucks was not on call but simply roamed the roadways on prescribed routes, rendering emergency mechanical repairs, including changing tires for women (but not for able-bodied men), and administering personal first aid.

In 1918 the Auto Club purchased three tow trucks for a pilot program that would become a permanent and well-loved benefit of membership. In August 1924, just after inaugurating the Highway Patrol, the Auto Club initiated Emergency Road Service, which allowed members to call for assistance, rather than awaiting the passage of a Highway Patrol vehicle.

When the Club launched the full-scale program, it had negotiated contracts with 120 garages throughout the thirteen counties served by the Club to provide emergency roadside service or towing a disabled vehicle without cost. Stranded motorists only had to present their Auto Club membership cards to settle payment for emergency services; in its first six months, 20,000 appreciative members called for help. Recognizing that its Emergency Road Service was popular with members, the Auto Club prepared this article explaining how to use this membership benefit.

Club employees circled this donut-shaped table to pick up individual sections to compile strip maps to destinations requested by members. Touring Bureau personnel answered half a million questions the year after the Auto Club moved into its new headquarters on West Adams and Figueroa and distributed more than seven million free maps.

Membership in the Auto Club rose nearly sevenfold between 1920 and 1930, to reach 137,698 before the economic freefall of the Great Depression caused that base to contract by more than 40 percent. The spacious and elegant public spaces at the new headquarters in downtown Los Angeles were the proving ground for the member services by which the Auto Club defined itself.

The sudden adoption of the automobile for individual transportation had dramatic effects on traffic flow and pedestrian safety in downtown Los Angeles. In 1920, 90 percent of the workers in downtown offices and businesses arrived by streetcar, but by 1924, nearly half used cars to get to work. The City Council attempted to relieve congestion by banning parking on downtown streets from 11 a.m. to 6 p.m. on weekdays, but the three rival newspapers and most of the downtown business community united in opposition to the measure, which was repealed less than three weeks after it passed in April 1920. The photo (right) was staged to show the hazards of cars to commuters, but that fact was not acknowledged in the caption, which suggested that this was a common occurrence: "Drunk drivers sometimes mow down a number of persons who are waiting in a 'Safety Zone' to board street cars."

The Automobile Club commissioned traffic engineers to study the problem of accommodating the growing number of cars. Their recommendations—effectively doubling the capacity of certain streets by making them one-way and envisioning a system of thoroughfares that would allow through traffic to circumvent the congested downtown district—were published in 1922 and inspired, in part, the Major Traffic Street Plan that was placed on the 1924 ballot. Voters approved that plan, along with $5 million to begin implementing it.

where streets could be crossed safely. The report also recommended that free-flowing arteries circle the city. The planners warned that:

"while many of the projects...may appear radical and prohibitive in cost, it should be borne in mind that Los Angeles, if it is to take its destined place among the great and beautiful cities of the world, must eventually make these improvements and the longer the delay the greater the ultimate cost."

In response, private parties interested in furthering comprehensive road projects formed the Los Angeles Traffic Commission and included Auto Club staff on its panel: general counsel David Faries and chief engineer Ernest East. The commission invited nationally prominent planners, among them Frederick Law Olmsted, Jr., to prepare a report. The commission published its *Major Traffic Street Plan for Los Angeles* in 1924 and created a vision for the city—new traffic regulations to promote greater efficiency of movement; the separation of through traffic from local traffic, streetcars from automobiles, rail lines from surface streets, widening of streets, and improved mass transit. The city attempted to make many of these improvements, but the vision of free-flowing traffic remained elusive.

The Auto Club also brought its road planning concerns to the state arena. Reacting to the sometimes shoddy condition of the new roads, the Auto Club advocated that roads be built to higher technical standards so they would last longer. It donated the services of consulting engineers to offer advice and sponsored the Road Confer-

The issue of attaining parity between the north and south in the allocation of highway construction resources came to a head in 1926 when the California State Automobile Association (CSAA), which represented motorists in the northern part of the state, and the Automobile Club of Southern California backed opposing measures on the state ballot. Both Measure 4, a gas tax increase supported by CSAA, and Measure 8, which the Auto Club asserted would keep "state highways out of politics" by reallocating existing state funds to build the same number of roads in both parts of the state, were soundly defeated by voters who may have been confused by the conflicting claims. That defeat brought both parties to the bargaining table in a spirit of compromise, which was articulated in the Breed Highway Bill of 1927 and was the basis of the state's highway policy for the next two decades.

A line of motorbikes bearing posters in support of Initiative 10 stands in the courtyard of the Auto Club headquarters. A banner trailed by a hybrid plane-helicopter, called an auto-gyro, confirms the Club's support of the measure, which advocated that all funds collected from gasoline taxes should be used for highway construction. This editorial from *Touring Topics* (October 1932) states the central premise that would be articulated in Initiative 10 on the state ballot in 1936:

"It has long since been determined in this state that those who use the roads and wear them out should pay for their maintenance and this has been accomplished by means of a gasoline tax. It also has been established in the minds of all fair-minded people that no money derived from motorists in the form of a gasoline tax should be diverted or used for any other purpose than that of road repair and improvement."

From 1927, when a bill authored by State Senator Arthur H. Breed established a gas tax to fund the state's first major road construction effort, California collected three cents on each gallon of gas purchased and another penny went to the federal government. In 1947 the Collier-Burns Highway Act increased the tariff paid to the state from three cents to 4.5 cents.

The November 1938 ballot included two provisions supported by the Auto Club. Measure 3, which continued the campaign to prevent, permanently, any diversion of gas tax revenues to projects other than road building, passed overwhelmingly. Measure 4, which recommended the creation of a single state highway authority to eliminate duplication between state and county road-building programs, was opposed by county governments and was defeated by the voters.

This Chrysler Airflow, first introduced in 1934, has seen a bit of touring if the many decals including French and German club insignias are an indication of its travels.

ence of County Highway Engineers in July 1920 at the California Club in Los Angeles.

Realizing the need for a comprehensive roadway plan, California Governor Friend W. Richardson appointed a Highway Advisory Committee in 1924, whose members included Ernest East, the Auto Club's chief engineer. The committee traveled the state highway system for a year, attended local meetings, talked to community members about their needs, and then submitted reports in 1925 with recommendations for road building.

One finding confirmed what many area residents believed: Southern California received less highway funding than the north. Ernest East pointed out that of the 6,400 miles of highways in the state system so far, 4,010 miles lay in the northern counties. The southern counties comprised approximately one-half of the area, taxable wealth, and population of the state, but had received only 34 percent of state highway expenditures. Armed with this information, the Auto Club began to work toward a more equitable outlay of state highway funds.

Finally, laws governing the operation of vehicles remained a tangled web of conflicting ordinances throughout California. J. Allen Davis, the Club's legislative counsel, helped draft the state's Motor Vehicle Act, which passed into law in 1923. This uniform vehicle code simplified California's motoring laws, helping to make roads throughout California safer.

Commuters drove longer distances to their jobs in the 1930s and cars were choking city streets, as this view of downtown Los Angeles from the middle of that decade shows. The Breed Highway Bill of 1933 funded a massive construction program to help the state's economy recover from lingering effects of the Depression and allocated 3,700 miles of secondary roads in Southern California—compared with 2,900 miles in the north—reaching the parity that had been a goal of Auto Club lobbying for more than a decade.

639898

PHIL T. HANNA,
2601 SO. FIGUEROA ST.,
LOS ANGELES, CALIF.

MEMBER **Automobile Club**
OF
Southern California

EXPIRES   PAYMENT
10-1-32   12 00

Harry J Bauer
PRESIDENT

Stanhold Mitchell
SECRETARY

Safety Programs Expand

As the number of highways and motorists grew, the Auto Club's opportunities for providing service to its members also expanded. One of the Auto Club's most popular efforts was its Highway Patrol Service, which began operation in 1924. The distinctive fleet of trucks, emblazoned with the Auto Club's logo and the motto "Good Samaritan of the Highway," patrolled highways from the Mexican border to Paso Robles, helping stranded motorists, patching and inflating tires, sweeping glass from the road, and directing traffic at congested intersections. The intrepid highway patrol drivers also reported auto thieves, recovered stolen tires, and provided directions for motorists who had lost their way. The patrol not only aided motorists, but also came to the rescue of hundreds of people affected when the Santa Clarita dam failed in 1925.

To augment the Highway Patrol Service, in the fall of 1924 the Auto Club authorized 119 garages in Southern California to provide towing services free of charge to members. The Highway Service Patrol program resulted from many years of careful planning, review of garage operations, and negotiation, and it was immediately popular with members. The Auto Club worked out reciprocal arrangements with the California State Automobile Association so that motorists were covered throughout the state.

As Westerners hit the road with their new auto-mobiles, campgrounds that also accommodated vehicles became increasingly common. During the 1920s, more permanent camps, which sheltered humans within structures and the prized cars under roofs, sprang up.

More cars and more people on the roads behind the wheel and walking meant more car crashes. Between 1930 and 1936, more than 150,000 people were killed or injured in automobile accidents in Los Angeles County (today about two thousand people a year are killed in traffic accidents, according to 1995 Los Angeles County Department of Health statistics). To help drivers operate their cars more safely and encourage pedestrians to stay out of the way, the Auto Club initiated its Safety Bureau in 1921. The Safety Bureau held assemblies for school children on pedestrian safety and in 1925 produced a public safety movie called "Why Be a Goose."

The Depression's Effects

Despite the Great Depression of the 1930s more and more motorists took to the roads and more people settled in California, seeking often-elusive dreams of finding work. Just before the stock market crash, Club membership in 1928 totaled 129,536, but in the next year, the phenomenal economic expansion of the 1920s ran out of gas. The Great Depression saw Auto Club membership drop by 44 percent and premiums written by the Interinsurance Exchange drop by 54 percent. The Club instituted a salary and hiring freeze and reduced membership fees. Club employees even donated one percent of their salaries to unemployment relief in Southern California.

This auto camp near San Diego, photographed in 1925, was a predecessor of the motels that would become ubiquitous along the nation's highways in the 1950s.

The Auto Club increased promotion to try to raise revenue, advertising in local newspapers and on the radio to entice members back.

Such programs expanded to include spots on local radio stations KFWB and KNX and direct mail campaigns. The 1932 Olympic Games provided a valuable opportunity for the Auto Club to make its services more broadly known to visitors attending the games. And as it would again in 1984, the Auto Club assisted in traffic planning and signposting for the games.

To promote membership and tourism, the Auto Club began an annual recreational equipment fair that featured the latest automobile models, gear for camping, fishing, and hunting, colorful mariachi bands, and demonstrations of outdoor sports. Models wore the latest fashions and braver attendees could compete in logrolling contests. The popular Outing Show, held in the courtyard of the headquarters building, became a major Southland event—attracting up to half a million participants— until it ended during World War II.

Despite the gloomy financial picture, the Auto Club assisted Southern California motorists in their quest for a larger portion of state highway funds, especially at a time when the federal and state governments launched massive construction programs to boost employment. Thanks in part to the efforts of Club representatives

The thoroughfares that were envisioned in the Auto Club's 1922 study and the 1924 Major Traffic Street Plan would be refined by the Auto Club's chief engineer Ernest East, using studies from 1930 and 1936, in the report (illustrated) that proposed the concept of freeways. East identified the one million intersections that subdivided the 11,000 miles of roads within Los Angeles County as "points of traffic conflict and hazard." He recommended limited-access motorways "for the exclusive use of motor vehicles" that would be interrupted neither with stop signs to regulate the in-flow of cars nor with rail crossings at grade. This ideal freeway was to be isolated by a three-to-one ratio of green space to roadway, a concept that can be seen in the divided highway that traversed Pomona in this photo from 1940, where the pastoral image of California was largely undisturbed by the road and visible from it.

The Arroyo Seco Parkway, seen (bottom) during construction and (top) after opening in 1940, wends through the dry riverbed—a flood control channel had been constructed to divert winter rains—where landmark cultural institutions like the Southwest Museum (visible on the horizon) had been built by an earlier generation. Such "parkways" embodied a nineteenth-century ideal of integrating an open landscape with the motorway. As other land uses encroached on the green buffer zone and some roadways were widened to accommodate the growing number of cars, parkways became less pastoral, a word few commuters would use to describe their daily drive on today's Pasadena Freeway.

TRAFFIC SURVEY

Los Angeles Metropolitan Area
1937

Engineering Department
Automobile Club of Southern California

An airplane view of the Olympic Stadium, Los Angeles, with the Swimming Stadium in the foreground. Here will be held the bulk of the events comprising the Tenth Olympiad, which is drawing renowned athletes from all parts of the world

THE OLYMPIC GAMES, *Ancient and Modern*

CONTESTS OF STRENGTH AND FLEETNESS, ALMOST 3000 YEARS OLD, COME TO PACIFIC COAST FOR FIRST TIME, JULY 30-AUGUST 14, 1932

By George R. Momyer

FROM Mount Erymanthus, in Western Greece, the river Alpheus comes tumbling down deep canyons to the Olympian plain. In its upper course it is ...

river god reflecting th...
fall. Burdened with t...
hides its face, and bu...
ples was built on its b...
with its throne of ced...
shrine of the ancient C...

A thousand years be...
primitive races that fre...
blue of their sky, flank...
there came into the liv...
acclaimed as the most c...

For their funeral cer...
dark river and cast asi...
and sports to speed th...
became tribal festivals...
games. Because of thei...
called Olympic games, a...
and the next was called...
tion was held in 776 B.C.

To 394 A.D. there was ...

"**T**he games will be of great future benefit to Southern California... because the contestants and other visitors will see the Southland for themselves and will carry to all parts of the world firsthand information about the Southland and its wonders," advised the editorial in the issue of *Touring Topics* that was current when the Tenth Olympiad opened in Los Angeles in the summer of 1932. It noted that routing inquiries for the region had increased 50 percent during April and May over the year previous and "these requests have in the past proved to be a reliable index of the volume of motor travel to Southern California."

"**M**iles of flower beds have been added to the rose borders that have made her [California's] highways famous," noted *Touring Topics*, citing as well more enduring improvements like construction of the stadiums for track and field and swimming events in Exposition Park (photo, top). The Olympics issue of the magazine featured an article on national parks of the West, which the Auto Club had helped make accessible to motor tourism and continued to promote. This message seems to have been taken to heart by its immediate constituency: "California cars rank second numerically in all of the national parks outside of California, being exceeded only by cars from the States in which the parks are located," *Touring Topics* announced in 1932, and it recommended a national parks itinerary for out-of-state visitors to the Los Angeles Olympics who could continue to tour the region.

---

from solid rock, 63.5 m.; and Hood River, 68.5 m.
If you're hungry, the Columbia Gorge Hotel just west of Hood River, is excellent; or, if you've started late from Portland, here's a splendid place to spend the night.
At Hood River, the loop road turns southerly, (just e. of town), to Mt.

Hood, 82.5 m.; Blue Bucket, 101 m.; and on to Government Camp and Battle Axe Inn, (suggested as a night stop), 117 m.
The road circles the e. and s. sides of prominent and beautiful Mt. Hood, (11,253 ft.). Score again for Capt. Vancouver, who named this peak for the same "Right Honorable Lord

Hood" whose name graces Hood Canal. The mountain was discovered by Lieut. Wm. Robert Broughton, an aide on the expedition, on Oct. 29, 1792. The first recorded ascent of the mountain occurred on Aug. 19, 1854. The peak has been climbed many times since, the most popular route being up the n.e. face.

Leaving Battle Axe Inn, (00.0 m.), the return route to Portland proceeds westerly to Rhododendron, 10 m.; Wemme, 13.5 m.; Cherryville, 22.5 m.; Sandy, 29.5 m.; Gresham, 41.5 m.; Portland, via Section Line Road, 54.5 m.
The total distance for this magnificent loop trip is 171.5 m.

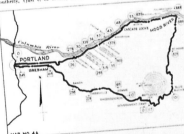

MAP NO. 4A

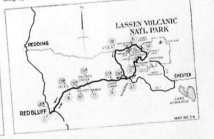

MAP NO. 5A

LASSEN VOLCANIC NATIONAL PARK

IT'S BEST to make the trip around Mt. Lassen (MAP 5A) in one day unless you're camping or willing to put up with primitive accommodations, for no modern hotels, as yet, are conveniently accessible in the park. The total distance is only 149.8 m. from Red Bluff around the mountain and back again to Red Bluff.
The route leads easterly from Red Bluff (00.0 m.), to Dales, 14 m., Elliott Ranch, 19.5 m.; Paynes Creek, 23 m.; Jiggs Camp, 36 m.; Mineral.

43 m. At Mineral (considerably e. of the park boundary) are located park headquarters. Here the route turns northward to the Mineral entrance checking station, 52 m. (The season is from June 1 to Oct. 30; Entrance fee, $1.)
Lassen Volcanic National Park was created Aug. 9, 1916, to protect the only active volcano in continental United States, hot springs, mud geysers, etc. Mt. Lassen, around which volcanic activity centers, (10,453 ft.), was discovered by Spanish explorers, attached to the Arguello expedition, in 1820. It was called Mt. San José. Later the peak was re-named for Peter Lassen, a pioneer of 1843, who secured a grant of land on Deer Creek, Tehama County, and who later operated the first steamer on the Sacramento River.
Mt. Lassen had been dormant for 200 years when, on May 30, 1914, it erupted, with smoke and ashes. Other major eruptions occurred on June 1, June 14, and Sept. 29 of the same year; and again (most violent) May 22, 1915. During the last eruption a

The Devastated Area of Lassen National Park, California, as it appears from Raker Mountain

veritable avalanche of mud poured down the north face in the vicinity of Hat Creek, completely devastating many thousands of acres.
From the Mineral entrance (52 m.) the road winds upward to Bumpass Hell (80 acres of active geysers), 58.5 m.; passes along the e. side of Helen Lake, skirts the s. side of the volcano, continues on to Summit Lake, 69 m., and then proceeds down through the devastated area of Hat and Lost Creeks, 77 m., to Manzanita and Reflection Lakes, 81 m. (excellent views of the volcano and of Chaos Crags). A stub-end road passes southward from Manzanita Lake to the very base of the volcano. Here is located the Loomis Museum (free to the public) containing photographs and relics of the volcano.
From Manzanita Lake the road passes westerly to Viola, 88 m. A modest but comfortable hotel is available here, operated by B. L. Loomis, a pioneer of the vicinity. If you want specific information about any point in the park, Loomis is eminently qualified to give it.

Turning southward at Viola, the road traverses the Lassen National Forest, rejoining the main highway again at Mineral, 106.8 m. From here one turns westerly, back to Red Bluff, 149.8 m.
The Boiling Lake (Lake Tartarus) and the Devil's Kitchen (if you're deeply interested) can be seen by passing easterly from Mineral (00.0 m.), to Chester, 30.5 m., thence north erly to Drakesbad, 48 m., the center of interest on the s. side of the peak.

Mt. Lassen, recently active California volcano, seen from across Manzanita Lake

YOSEMITE NATIONAL PARK

GIVE two days at the very least to Yosemite (MAP 5B); as much more as you can. Leaving Manteca (00.0 m.), the route into Yosemite National Park via Big Oak Flat passes due e. through Escalon, 12.5 m. (Sp.—"stepping stone"), to Oakdale, 22 m. Here it crosses the Stanislaus River, passing on to Knight's Ferry, 34 m., and thence to Chinese Camp, 51.5 m.
This region is redolent of the golden days of '49. It is the center of the Mother Lode group of placer mines extended from Mormon Bar, in

here), the road drops into the canyon of Wood's Creek and on to Jacksonville, 56 m. At 58.7 m. the route crosses the Tuolumne River over the historic Stevens Bar bridge and begins the long ascent over the Priest grade (average grade 4.5%) to Priests, 65 m., and Big Oak Flat, 66 m. The point takes its name from a large oak tree (11 ft. in diameter) that formerly stood here. At 68 m., Groveland is reached. In the days of '49 Groveland was known as First Garrotte, from a man who was garrotted there. Two miles e. of Groveland (70 m.), was the site of Second Garrotte, made famous in Bret Harte's renowned poem, *Tennessee's Partner*.
Continuing easterly the road passes through Buck Meadows, 79 m., Carl Inn, 93.5 m. (a popular resort and the junction of the road across the Sierra to Mono Lake and Lake Tahoe via Tioga Pass), and reaches the Tuolumne Grove of Big Trees at 99 m. (a privately owned group of *Sequoia gigantea*, containing the Pride of California and the largest of the so-called "tunnel trees," the *Dead Giant*, more than 100 ft. in circumference).
A short distance beyond the Tu...

To the Floor of the Valley—Yosemite National Park embraces an area of 1126 sq. mi., straddling the crest of the Sierra Nevada and including some of the most magnificent mountain scenery in the world. Yosemite Valley proper, where the tourist's interest centers, occupies but 8 sq. mi. of the total area. Leaving Crane Flat a ridge is crossed (7100 ft.), Tamarack Flat (liberally sprinkled with tamaracks or lodge pole pines (*Pinus contorta*), is traversed, and Gentry's Ranger Station is reached at 108 m. One-way traffic only is permitted on the road from Gentry's to the floor of the valley, owing to its narrowness and the heavy grades (15-20%). Cars ... the valley on the odd ...

TOURING TOPICS

JULY 1932

20¢

OLYMPIC VILLAGE

OLYMPIC FINE ARTS MUSEUM

OLYMPIC STADIUM

ROSE BOWL

SWIMMING STADIUM

Oxnard

Pasadena

Los Angeles

Pacific Ocean

San Pedro

Long Beach

Xth OLYMPIAD LOS ANGELES 1932

The International Pacific Highway, a roadway that would extend from Fairbanks, Alaska, to Buenos Aires, linking coastal states with neighbors to the north and south, was a grandiose plan for an era of financial adversity, but it had been launched to thwart a proposed Pan-American Highway through Texas that business leaders feared could divert trade and tourism away from the West Coast. Harry Chandler had suggested a highway linking North and South America along the Pacific and published a map and story about the proposal in the *Los Angeles Times* in August 1929.

The first pathfinding expedition, consisting of eight engineers and cartographers from the Auto Club, accompanied by a reporter from the *Los Angeles Times*, left Los Angeles in five Fords on March 15, 1930. Their goal was to survey a sector in northern Mexico—between the border at Nogales, Arizona, and Mexico City—of the proposed 12,000-mile route. The published report noted the challenging terrain but concluded with a hopeful statement of what South America could expect from the project: "Road construction in the United States and elsewhere has hastened development, increased productivity, reduced transpor-

tation costs, given employment, and in short created prosperity." The motivation for the United States was also noted: "It can reasonably be expected with good roads existing that the volume of trade with our neighbors, especially to the South, will be enormously increased to our mutual benefit."

In the same month that the first expedition returned to Los Angeles, another group headed north on an 828-mile journey from Vancouver to Hazelton. The Second International Pacific Highway Expedition, which continued the proposed route south from Mexico City to San Salvador, undertook an arduous journey in the winter and spring of 1931. Six veterans of the first expedition led this effort, but the road conditions were even more challenging, forcing the crew to simply hack a trail through a wild landscape for much of the 1,400-mile route. Switchbacking through the narrow gorge of the Tehuantepec River entailed fording the river more than one hundred times.

The Auto Club remained optimistic in the Second Expedition report it published, but other factors prevented the project from ever receiving the unified international effort needed for its realization.

Ernest East, Henry Keller, Carl McStay, and J. Allen Davis, Southern Californians received a more equitable allotment of gasoline-tax funds for new state highway construction from the 1933 Breed bill.

In spite of the years of planning, the continued influx of residents meant that congestion was still a problem. In 1937, the Auto Club initiated a survey of the roads and their use. It reported that the population of Los Angeles County had climbed above 2,690,000, and the number of automobiles registered in Los Angeles County totaled more than 960,000, 40.6 percent of all the cars in the state.

Analyzing the data from traffic counts in 1930 and 1936, the Club's engineer Ernest East asserted that "the relation which formerly existed between home and place of occupation has almost, if not completely, disappeared." East envisioned limited access roadways that allowed commuters to move freely around the city without being hindered by intersections and railroad crossings. He imagined these roadways landscaped with greenbelts through suburban areas so that a flavor of Southern California's scenic beauty would be preserved.

East's report joined a growing stream of plans and recommendations that moved toward creation of a regional freeway network. The first piece was the building of the Arroyo Seco Parkway between downtown Los Angeles and Pasadena as well as a

IN THIS ISSUE
ZORRA—NOTES ON THE LIFE OF A DOMESTICATED GRAY FOX
AKARA, NAPOLEON OF THE DESERT   FAITHFUL COUPLE, A SHORT STORY OF THE SOUTHLAND
THREE "MOTOR-GRAPHS" THROUGH SCENIC SOUTHERN CALIFORNIA

Touring Topics
November 1922

More Than 72,000
Copies This Issue

AUTOMOBILE CLUB OF SOUTHERN C.
GOOD ROADS

Mitten Buttes
Located in Monument Valley, Northern Arizona
Painted by Charles Hamilton Owens

TOURING TOPICS
DECEMBER 1933 IN TWO PARTS: PART 1   20 CENTS A COPY

IN THIS ISSUE
Winners in Touring Topics Name Contest
EMERALDS NEXT TO THE SKY   LIFE BENEATH A DESERT JOSHUA
"COOL, WINE-HUED GRAPES BREATHE FRAGRANCES"

Although the Auto Club's magazine had flourished under the skilled editorship of Phil Townsend Hanna since 1926, it was an optional subscription, for which members paid an additional fee. As the Depression lingered, *Touring Topics* subscriptions dropped even faster than membership renewals. To ensure that members would not miss information essential to availing themselves of services the Club offered, a separate publication was sent gratis to all members after 1932. Thus relieved of imparting such information, the magazine was allowed to become "a literate showcase of the West, its history, its problems and its aspirations, its people, its wildlife and its landscapes," in the words of Patrice Manahan who worked with Hanna and succeeded him as the publication's editor.

one-mile section of freeway over Cahuenga Pass, between Hollywood and the San Fernando Valley. Both of these stretches of highway opened within a few days of each other in 1940. Because World War II intervened, however, almost no additional freeways would be built until the late 1940s.

Touring Topics Becomes *Westways*

One powerful tool to retain members, as well as a bright spot in the economic gloom, was the success of the Auto Club's membership magazine, *Touring Topics*. When Phil Townsend Hanna became editor of *Touring Topics* in 1926, he brought with him a vision of Southern California's land, history, and people that belied the stereotype of a cultural wasteland. Hanna moved in Southern California's literary and cultural circles and the Club had the means to pay artists and writers for their work at a time when they had few other sources of income. He hired such well-known writers, artists, and photographers as Carey McWilliams, M.F.K. Fisher, Edward Weston, William Saroyan, and Maynard Dixon.

The magazine became known especially for its vibrant cover art, using the work of artists who had been attracted to California's varied terrain, mild climate, and un-

Rare Edition

By Ward Ritchie
Illustrations by Paul Landacre

INDIO MOUNTAINS

THE STORY of Paul Landacre is one of triumph and heartbreak. He was born in Columbus, Ohio, on July 9, 1893. As a handsome young boy, athletically inclined, he became the premier scholastic miler in Ohio, easily winning the state meet. As an athlete with great promise he was wooed by many colleges but decided to attend his hometown Ohio State University. As a freshman in 1914 and 1915 he continued to run and to win. Then he was struck down with an obscure fever, which at the time baffled his physician and left him crippled for life with a stiff leg and a feeling of great depression. He quit the university in 1916 and for therapy began to draw, for which he always had a natural talent.

He left Ohio for California, coming to San Diego. He hoped to make a living as a commercial artist. It is doubtful he was too successful,

being stubborn and opinionated, as well as a perfectionist. But he did meet a girl, Margaret McCreery, who was working as a copywriter in one of the local advertising agencies. I had known her brother who had been captain of the Stanford football team while I was there. She was a hearty girl, lovely and sweet-tempered. Landacre was handsome and aesthetic despite his infirmities. They were married and theirs was a love that lasted in intimate harmony for almost forty years. She devoted herself to him.

Once, when being interviewed, he was asked what Margaret did. He thought for a moment and answered, "She takes care of the correspondence, answers the telephone, is chancellor of the exchequer, drives me to and from wherever I have to go, helps push the lever of the press when I have to print a large block, delivers prints,

checks the manuscript when I am illustrating a book, keeps house and is an excellent cook. And then she acts as a critic and a balance wheel; she boosts my morale when I'm discouraged and calms me if I get too excited over my work at the wrong time. Any art coming out of this studio is a dual production for sure."

She did much more than this. She warmed his frail body at night. She built his confidence. She worked for their food while he was learning the greatness which was to be his. It was as close and as beautiful an association as I have ever known.

A good many years ago I thought I'd write something about the Landacres. I began one night:

"Paul and Margaret Landacre live a couple of hills over from Silver Lake which separates us. Their house, like a redwood dam, lies on a

16

ILLUSTRATIONS AND PHOTOGRAPH COURTESY OF J. M. LANDACRE

By 1934 the magazine's title seemed outdated: "touring" suggested a grand excursion to an exotic location and in that economically pinched era, the increasingly common automobile served more prosaic functions. The Auto Club held a contest, offering a $500 prize for the winning title, *Westways*, which was selected by the board of directors. "Tides West," the runner-up, became the title of a monthly column by Carey McWilliams, a lawyer and reporter for the *Los Angeles Times*; the themes of this column were later incorporated in *Southern California: An Island on the Land*, which remains a landmark history of the region. Paul Landacre, whose woodblock prints evoked California's rough-hewn landscape, was profiled in an article by Ward Ritchie, whose Plantin Press set standards for fine typography and book printing in the West.

usual landforms. Artists made use of impressionist and realistic techniques; the humor of daily life and the beauty of California's mountains, deserts, forests, and coastlands as subjects; and media as diverse as pen and ink, watercolor, oil, and photography.

The Auto Club's administration recognized Hanna's efforts: "The policy of presenting prehistoric, historic, and contemporary stories of the Southwest," wrote the Club's out-going president Edward Lyman in his annual report for 1929, brought "a wider and more appreciative audience than ever before." To reflect the magazine's broadened scope, a contest was held among members to rename it in 1934. It bears the winning name—*Westways*—to this day. Hanna noted that the name reflected "the romance, adventure, unexcelled scenic attractions, geographical wonderlands, artists, scientists, musicians, and authors who are doing things in a big way—the essence of California."

FRIEZE. *Sheltered by an overhanging rock ledge a row of sculptured figures extends along the top of a wall. Wherever there is protection from the wind, the carved forms are less smooth, and have the appearance of dampened clay*

SEEING CALIFORNIA WITH EDWARD WESTON

Red Rock Can[yon]

TWENTY-SIX miles north of Mojave on th[e]
ley Highway a spur of the Tehachapi
one side, and a corresponding point of
shuts in Death Valley on the west, almost
to pinch out the narrow pass called Red Roc[k]

Justly famed for its extravagantly eroded
colored formations, Red Rock Canyon is a s[o]
ending delight for photographers and desert

The rocky walls have been carved and gou[ged]
into countless weird and varied forms, and n[a]
tion has given these shapes names no less
the shapes themselves. Praying nuns, gargoy[les]
temples and palaces of all kinds, heads of
sters, are all to be seen.

Only twice has the spot figured prominent[ly]
In 1849 the Manly party passed through it,
ship and horror in Death Valley. In 19[0]
Bishop, a modest, patient and cheerful hom[e]
discovered mines in the vicinity that catap[ult]
tunes from the poverty of homesteading t[o]
ease and luxury of considerable wealth.

MAGUEY, TEXCOCO   Edward Weston, 1926

THE PHOTOGRAPHY OF EDWARD WESTON
BY MERLE ARMITAGE

ONE does not need to be familiar with modern movements in art to enjoy the work of Edward Weston but one can understand him much more profoundly and can more fully appreciate the subtle nuance of his photographs if one knows something of the aims of the modernists. Weston might easily be called "a realist." He places his camera before an object—almost any object in fact—for he ranges from shells to green peppers, from Mexican pyramids to bathrooms. His camera lense takes in every detail before it, with no diffusion and with a hard and sharp, almost a piercing, intensity.

It would be perfectly proper to assume that almost anyone with a fine camera could go this far. The thing which distinguishes the work of Weston from that of any other I have seen is entirely one of approach. Weston is interested in achieving that subtle essence of a subject which is the aim of many artists of the modern French school. Almost anything has some significant character. Take for example that old picture with which we are all familiar: "The Three Graces." I have not seen a reproduction of this for years, yet it left on my memory a certain impression. Last year, Picasso, with an economy of drawing suggestive of shorthand, drew "The Three Graces." As compared with the old elaborate and faithfully photographic, "The Three

Graces," it was simply a few lines representing the three women. But what a revelation! The essential quality of this work was preserved and even accentuated but the unnecessary paraphernalia with which the old work was weighed down, was cut away as with a knife.

I am not attempting to explain Picasso but this is certainly one of his qualities. So it is with Weston. He takes, not simply a photograph of something, he takes that something's essential character, if I may be permitted a banal phrase.

As most photographers approach a subject from a standpoint of fine photography, of unusual angles for a "shot," of surface composition, I should say that Weston approaches it from the angle of revealing its true content, its natural decorativeness or design, its most significant form. The difference is not of mechanics so much as of mentality. The natural formations of ship's masts, of a grouping of chairs, of the human body, of rocks, of tree-trunks, are revealed anew to us through Weston's camera, setting forth with startling clearness the individuality and the unlikeness of each. Although there is never the slightest resorting to "tricks" or to "faking," there is a strangeness about all Weston's conceptions, which is common to all great Art

RUMPLES. *Worn smooth by the wind and cut deep by watercourses, this miniature mountain-range looks like a heap of rippled satin. It has a pale gray-green color and stands at the end of a small side-canyon, blocking it up*

"**A**s a matter involving pleasure, health and profit it might well be recommended to the citizens of California that they give themselves the advantage of seeing their own state thoroughly in order that they may enjoy their own highways and their own scenic beauties," one of the last issues of *Touring Topics* suggested, citing statistics that showed that 62 percent of the cars crossing the California border already bore California plates, and "have presumably been making recreation tours of other states."

From 1937 the monthly feature "Seeing California with Edward Weston" showed *Westways* readers an inspired vision of their state's beauty and established a high profile for fine art photography. The Trip of the Month (opposite) was another format for boosting tourism, a perennial goal of the magazine that is expressed in styles particular to each era.

8

Designs and Patterns in Ribbons of Concrete

PHOTOGRAPHS BY DAVID MUENCH

• Concrete pillars support the Long Beach Freeway at the point where it crosses the Santa Ana Freeway.

• Above, looking toward the Vine Street off-ramp, the Hollywood Freeway is carpeted with headlight streaks. Downtown Hollywood is at the right.

• Below is the four-level interchange, where the Pasadena, Harbor, San Bernardino, Hollywood freeways weave together and out again.

• Below, the calm of a sunlit Sunday morning settles over the interchange of the Santa Ana and Long Beach freeways.

COLOR
om AUTUMN'S
PALETTE

Photographs by ANSEL ADAMS

• The Giant California black oaks which dot Yosemite's valley floor are an inspiring sight in full autumn splendor.

Transplanted Easterners who suffer a nostalgic twinge for "back home" when the first frosts herald the advent of Fall will discover an acceptable substitute on both slopes of the High Sierra during October and November.

In few places in the West is the change of seasons so evident and more beautiful than in Yosemite National Park. Here the flaming hues of red, yellow and gold on the maples, oaks, dogwoods and cottonwoods transform the floor of the valley into a veritable bowl of color. To make the scene unforgettable the brilliant colors combine with the contrasting gray and white cliffs, the green conifers and the golden-brown meadows. Here, and over on the Inyo-Mono slopes, Nature is in her best holiday dress. Don't miss it this year!

• Rugged Half Dome, above, furnishes a majestic backdrop for the brilliant color along the highway
• Sombre gray walls of granite, centers are a striking contrast to golden yellow of the oaks and cottonwoods
• Vivid spots of color against white of North Dome and its evergreen base, right, provide a spectacular setting for early morning canters

26

Ansel Adams, whose images of the matchless landscape of the West revealed the complete range of tones in black and white photography, is represented by a selection of monochrome pictures that reveal the "Colors of Autumn's Palette."

Father and son Josef and David Muench were among the photographers who adapted the best tradition of nature and landscape photography to rapidly improving color film. This 1959 article in *Westways* reveals an aspect of David Muench's work—black-and-white studies of graphic patterns in man-made forms—that has since been eclipsed by his resonant color compositions of nature's beauty.

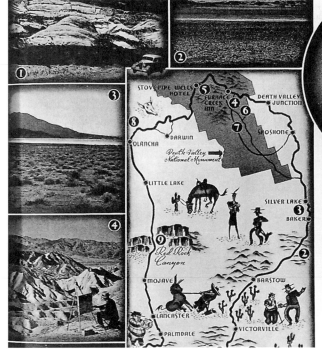

Westways
"TRIP OF THE MONTH"
Death Valley

What to See:

1 Sandstone outcroppings near the summit of Cajon Pass mark the location of the San Andreas fault, California's longest rift, the movements of which have caused many a major earthquake

2 The Devil's Playground, scintillating terraces of white, drifting sand-dunes south of Baker, form a striking contrast to the vividly-colored mountain ranges around them in several directions

3 Silver Lake is typical of the dry lakes of the desert—snowlike in summer when its alkaline surface is exposed; gleaming when filled with winter rains

4 Zabriskie Point, overlooking the brilliant eroded canyons along Death Valley's eastern side, commands an inspiring view. Favored

Another initiative begun in 1934 to increase awareness of the Auto Club, and so perhaps its membership, were exhibitions of recreational vehicles and outdoor equipment. These so-called Outing Shows, held each spring from 1934 to 1941, transformed the courtyard of Auto Club headquarters with displays of the latest trailers as well as camping, hunting, and fishing gear. Models paraded through the crowd wearing the latest outfits for outdoor sports; police experts demonstrated sharpshooting and target practice. There were logrolling contests and prizes for the woodsman whose axe bisected a redwood stump in the least amount of time. Attendance was counted at 66,000 for the first Outing Show, but nearly half a million people thronged the last of the shows, which were not reinstated after World War II.

Poster, circa 1942, was one of a series installed on billboards around Club headquarters to encourage workers who remained stateside during the war to view their efforts with the same dedication as did military personnel.

The Auto Club applied its expertise in devising safety training programs for Red Cross and military personnel who would be called on to drive unfamiliar large vehicles in difficult terrain in wartime service.

STAY ON THE JOB AND FINISH THE JOB!

AUTOMOBILE CLUB OF SOUTHERN CALIFORNIA

The Auto Club funded military efforts by buying $3.4 million in U.S. War Bonds. Employee purchases totaled a half million; membership dues and fees collected through the Interinsurance Exchange made up the balance of the investment in bonds.

4
"Grown up with the Automobile"

1940–1965

KEEP BUYING WAR BONDS

6th WAR LOAN

AUTOMOBILE CLUB OF SOUTHERN CALIFORNIA

"Frankly, the whole gasoline rationing business strikes me as unnecessary. I own a car. I know just what my tires are good for. I know I can't get any more tires. I know that if I abuse my tires I shall have to lay my car up for the duration. If I am fool enough to abuse my tires, under such circumstances, it is not gasoline rationing I need. It is a bunk in an insane asylum...."
—Member G. E. Kenley to Standish Mitchell, Club Secretary

On the Home Front

WHEN JAPANESE FIGHTERS BOMBED the naval base at Pearl Harbor in Hawaii in December 1941, the Auto Club had begun emerging from the Depression as a lean and efficient organization, focusing on its core mission of service to its members. Those services, it discovered, proved very useful in the upcoming war effort.

At the outset of World War II, motorists throughout the United States relied on the Auto Club for its detailed and accurate maps. Because of this, the cartography department devoted all of its time to military projects. Not only did it donate thousands of maps of Southern California for service men and women to use, but it generated new and more specialized maps. In the interest of defending the coast and the many military installations in such places as Long Beach, San Pedro, Oceanside, and inland in the desert, the cartography department prepared detailed maps. These showed emergency landing fields as well as maps of railroads, telephone lines, major highways, bridges, and tunnels that could prove problematic if damaged—especially for troop deployment and evacuation.

The signposting department prepared to mark evacuation routes. The Club created and posted three hundred "Coast Guard Alert" signs along the coast.

The cartography and signposting divisions of the Auto Club devoted most of their time to the war effort, preparing maps for troop deployment and evacuation routes, as well as installing signs at military bases (above left).

The nation's rubber supply had been curtailed by the war in the Pacific, so salvage campaigns were begun to recycle existing material (above right). The Auto Club programs collected forty tons of rubber, much of it from old inner tubes.

The department also posted 7,500 signs along coast roads reminding motorists to dim their lights to keep shipping and coastal areas from illumination at night. By the end of the war, the signposting department had placed 24,000 signs at military installations and information centers for service people.

The Auto Club's tireless campaigning for good roads had paid off. It provided General George S. Patton's staff with advice and expertise in building roads through difficult terrain. The Auto Club had experience in planning roads through desert areas, and this was knowledge that proved useful to Patton's troops and tanks in North Africa. The Club's Public Safety Department also trained military drivers as well as Red Cross personnel in safe driving techniques and auto repair.

Just as in World War I, the Auto Club bought scores of U.S. War Bonds and encouraged employees and members to buy them too. The Club's "Give Them a Lift" campaign provided rides to military men and women on leave in Southern California and gave members a vehicle for becoming a more active part of the war effort. By 1942 more than 28,000 drivers had volunteered to transport service personnel.

The Club also supported rationing and voluntary conservation efforts—such as the "Keep it Under 40" program to lower speed limits and thereby minimize use of gasoline, tires, and automobiles—and taught basic car maintenance to extend the

The Auto Club posted names of employees who had entered military service. A photograph of three employees wearing uniforms of various branches of the armed services illustrated both the list of Club servicemen, and a poster promoting a program in which civilian volunteers offered transportation to military personnel. The "Give Them a Lift" program had already been in operation for a few months when America entered World War II, but the restrictions prohibiting nonessential travel and rationing gas and tires added new urgency to this effort. The Auto Club promoted the service with posters and decals for car windshields that identified participants. Entertainment industry figures like Bob Hope brought a high profile to such efforts, which involved 28,000 automobile owners at its peak.

automobiles' usefulness.

"Whereas for forty years the Club has taken the lead in encouraging the volume and radius of travel for business and recreation, it became necessary almost overnight to discourage all but essential motoring," president Harry Bauer noted ironically in the 1943 annual report.

Some Club members, such as G. E. Kenley quoted above, were irate about rationing. Club directors preferred voluntary conservation to rationing, but Club Secretary Standish Mitchell responded to Kenley:

> "It is a necessary war measure, and as such I feel it is the Club's patriotic duty to help it succeed and to counsel against open protest until it has had a fair time of trial and adjustment. I also feel it will be our equally patriotic duty to watch it carefully, and when and if it undeniably foretells economic chaos, to protest to and insist on relief from the highest authority in the land. You may be sure we will do just that."

Ten percent of the nation's war industry centered in the Los Angeles area, and the new defense jobs brought with them an influx of people and their cars; 85 percent of them, one study showed, traveled to work by car. New residents meant new members, but military priorities and rationing meant no new cars were available, and membership and the number of insurance policies began to drop. The number of

The war effort stopped freeway construction. The Arroyo Seco Parkway and Cahuenga Pass had been completed before the war. But surveys had shown that three-quarters of Southern Californians relied on private transportation and with the population boom that was anticipated, correctly, in the postwar years, the region could suffer from the disparity between the number of motorists and the amount of limited-access roadways.

The Auto Club participated from 1944 with other business and government groups on the California Major Highways Committee, which formulated state policy on these issues. Its recommendations—increasing the gasoline tax and vehicle registration fees to fund road construction—were eventually incorporated in the Collier-Burns Highway Act, which was approved in June 1947. Federal legislation that same year provided for 2,000 miles of urban freeways.

accidents rose—cars were older and roads were not maintained—causing insurance costs to rise. Gains caused by the booming economy and population following the war offset these loses, aided by the high profile given to the Auto Club's efforts. As General Counsel J. Allen Davis later noted, "the astonishing increase in membership...is conclusive evidence of the all-out war-time service by the Club."

Cutting through the Smog

War industries and the region's many new residents had altered the environment. Air pollution and the complicated web of causes leading to it would have an enormous impact on the Auto Club and motorists in the coming decades. When the first terrifying blankets of smog clouded Los Angeles in 1943, however, scientists and city planners alike were uncertain what caused it—after all, there had always been haze and fog in the Los Angeles basin. Newspapers and scientists blamed rubber plants and other industries, but after the city and county adopted measures to curb emissions from these factories, air pollution remained a significant problem.

In 1946 the county and city of Los Angeles adopted smoke abatement ordinances. In

The late 1940s car overlooking a desert landscape (opposite) marked with the interlocking patterns of a freeway exchange symbolizes the new access that motorists experienced in this period. This tent-car hybrid (above) is a 1948 Nash 600 Super, which would not have been atypical of the vehicles that allowed postwar populations to enjoy Southern California's mild winter climate in desert auto camps (right).

Westways cover girls of the 1940s personified the natural beauty of California and were often juxtaposed with maps or icons of its scenic treasures. Female motorists took to the highways in greater numbers in the 1940s after many women began driving because spouses were absent in the military.

1947 the state created the Los Angeles Air Pollution Control District. From the late 1940s through the late 1950s, the Air Pollution Control District focused on cutting emissions from oil refineries, metal industries, and the smudge pots of citrus groves, which were still numerous throughout the area. These measures cut some of the air pollution in the area, but it soon became evident that auto emissions were a major source of pollution.

The Auto Club began its own investigations, and in 1954, J. Allen Davis and director Asa Call helped to establish the privately funded Air Pollution Foundation at the University of Southern California. Based on research, standards were promulgated for air quality in the late 1950s. The Motor Vehicle Pollution Control Board was established by the California legislature in 1960. The board, which included a representative of the Auto Club, set standards for automotive pollution control devices, tested prototypes, and certified those devices that met the standards. That year, auto manufacturers began voluntary installation of pollution control devices on all new cars. These crankcase ventilation devices were simple, reliable, and effective, reducing

emissions by approximately 30 percent. By 1965 the state required the devices on all new cars and on specified retrofits for used cars depending on their age.

Better and Better Service

As early as 1943, the Auto Club began to study how the organization would make a transition to a postwar era. Executive staff such as Stan Mitchell, Phil Hanna, Ernest East, Don Doig, and J. Allen Davis determined that the Auto Club's tried and true formula was best: "Better and better service in established fields with the addition of new services as required to meet the needs of our members."

Even if the mission didn't change, growth of membership required new levels of infrastructure for service delivery at the same time that a transition to a new generation of leadership was beginning. Many members of the executive staff such as Standish Mitchell, Ernest East, J. Allen Davis, and Phil Hanna had served since the 1910s and 1920s, and the same was true of staff at all levels. The end of World War II also brought many new and returning employees to the Club. To help fit in as seamlessly as possible, the Auto Club produced a manual, *You...and the Club*.

"We are proud of the large number of Club employees who have been associated with us for 10, 20, 30 and more years. These are the nucleus of our large family, veterans of service who

Crowds in Auto Club headquarters on the final day in 1957 when annual car registration could be filed. The Club had trained personnel and provided office space for this service beginning in 1911. By the 1950s in its role assisting the Department of Motor Vehicles, the Club collected and transmitted millions of dollars annually in licensing fees, and provided a convenient service to those members who didn't procrastinate in availing themselves of it.

achieved their positions not only though personal efficiency, but also because other employees willingly shared with them their knowledge and skill. In turn, they would like to help you."

In a move to further serve its members, the Auto Club healed its breach with the American Automobile Association. Members would have access to more services as they traveled out of state and even in other countries. As the largest auto club affiliated with the AAA, the Automobile Club of Southern California gained a strong role in its executive council and an important means for influencing federal highway development policy.

Fiftieth Anniversary Celebration

In 1950 the Auto Club celebrated its fiftieth anniversary, by re-creating the 1903 and 1904 test runs to the east end of the county, driving thirty-seven classic cars from Los Angeles to Redlands for the occasion. *Westways* published a special edition tracing the history of the automobile in Southern California. It included "The Wheel and the Bell," an account by editor Phil Townsend Hanna of the Auto Club's history. California and its people had "grown with the automobile," and the vibrant car culture for which the region is known began to bloom. Buildings meant to attract drivers whirring by had been built since the 1920s, but drive-throughs, drive-ins, and motels began to appear everywhere. Southern Californians, prosperous as never before, de-

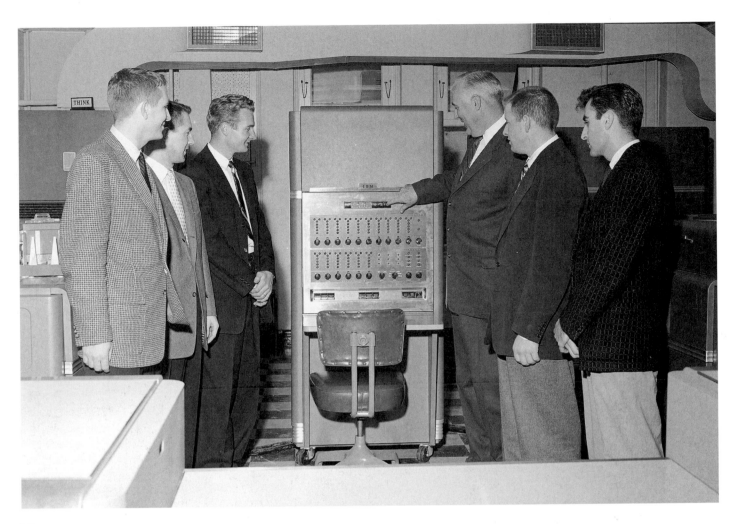

The IBM 650, a 3.5-ton computer, was state of the art when it was installed in March 1957. The machine handled 78,000 additions or subtractions per minute or 5,000 multiplications or 3,500 divisions per minute, allowing the Auto Club to deliver its services more efficiently.

The SigAlert is a distinctly Southern California phenomenon that identifies an accident or other situation that affects freeway traffic patterns for more than a half hour. Its name derives from that of Lloyd Sigmon, a local radio announcer who broadcast his first such announcement on September 5, 1955, requesting that medical personnel among his listeners respond to a train-automobile collision. SigAlert was adopted as a proper noun in the regional dialect: it is so labeled on this traffic monitor at the Los Angeles Police Department Regional Traffic Center.

An employee from the Club's Touring Bureau uses a machine to measure distances between two locations, illuminated on the map behind him, presumably to help a member calculate travel time.

The "four-level," an exchange that links the 110 and 101 freeways downtown, was designed between 1941 and 1944 when two segments of those freeways were the only such existing roadways in Los Angeles. Because of space constrictions at this already urbanized intersection, engineers stacked the entrance and exit ramps rather than arranging them in a full cloverleaf configuration. Heralded as an engineering marvel when construction was completed in 1950, it is commonly seen as a symbol of the Southland's congested freeways a half century later.

The growing complexity of the region's infrastructure is reflected in the size of this composite map.

"California at the Crossroads"

1965–1990

"Automobiles and highways have played major roles in California's unparalleled development and prosperity. They have helped us achieve a way of life envied throughout the world—a way of life based upon the priceless asset of mobility: the freedom to go where and when we desire, the flexibility to live, work and play where we wish. Never has the well-being of so many been so directly dependent upon the unhampered turning of the wheel."
—CLUB EXECUTIVE VICE PRESIDENT JOSEPH HAVENNER, 1966 ANNUAL REPORT

Challenges Ahead

IN FEBRUARY 1971, the Los Angeles Cultural Heritage Board declared the Auto Club's headquarters building "Historical Monument No. 72," one of the finest remaining examples of the Spanish colonial style. The Hunt and Burns structure, augmented by seventy-eight district offices, had functioned well for the Auto Club for half a century, and the community identified the majestic building with the Auto Club's long tradition of service to its members. To house its expanding staff and keep pace with Southern California's continued growth, the Auto Club began to renovate the building and added a four-story addition along Adams Boulevard.

"But growth," noted an April 1970 issue of the member newsletter, *Auto Club News Pictorial*, "brings problems—and we will face some important ones in the 1970s." In the mid-1960s, the Auto Club had much to look forward to—the highway system continued to expand, with 500 of nearly 1,500 planned miles open and in use. However, increasing inflation as the 1960s gave way to the 1970s meant that costs for highway construction escalated rapidly, and plans for expanding the freeway system were scaled back. Only 800 of the planned 1,500 miles were built. Residents began to question the costs to neighborhoods to make way for freeways and to worry about air pollution. Congestion on the freeways and streets made many wish for alternatives to traveling by automobile. By the early 1970s nearly every resident of Southern Califor-

YOU'RE ONLY
A FOOT
FROM TROUBLE

Check your Brakes

Waves roll to the shoreline and a message from the Auto Club trails above a Southern California beach: "Drive home carefully...Live and let live."

This poster, circa 1945, reminded motorists about a simple step for monitoring an important safety device: check your brakes.

nia was a member of the motoring public, and this public had diverse views about what was best for themselves and their communities.

Proposition 18, a proposal on the November 1970 ballot that would permit the use of gasoline tax funds for mass transit uses, reflected these points of view. Despite seeming widespread support, surveys of the Auto Club membership indicated that while a majority agreed that mass transit should supplement highway construction, they felt that gas taxes should be used for highway use only. In the end, voters narrowly defeated the proposition.

Increases in fuel costs and a shortage of gasoline compounded the community's frustration with car travel. The oil embargo of 1973 inaugurated gas lines and gas rationing that persisted intermittently into the late 1970s. The Auto Club urged members to reduce fuel consumption, but it fretted in its *Pictorial* that "compliance with emission and air quality regulation...could well result in disaster for all Southern Californians." The Auto Club advocated for "realistic standards and an attainable time frame within which to achieve them." Southern California residents increasingly purchased more fuel-efficient automobiles, often guided by Auto Club reports in its publications.

The Auto Club helped evaluate alternatives to individuals driving alone on freeways—including minibus service through downtown Los Angeles and carpooling. Throughout its history the Club looked to engineering and technology for solutions

The Auto Club produces a wide variety of brochures to accompany its ongoing safety programs.

Henry Cheshire, who served as Auto Club President from 1973 to 1987, was concerned about growing traffic congestion in Southern California. He pushed for efficient use of new and existing freeways.

to the problems of urban growth and it continued to do so. It supported legislation authorizing emission-control devices on new cars in the late 1960s based on research conducted at its Automobile Research and Diagnostic Center. Club engineers evaluated alternative fuels, including diesel and natural gas, as well as possible future solutions, such as electric and hybrid cars; its Automotive Research Center became a testing facility for government agencies and private industry. The Club also helped launch Commuter Computer to match up carpoolers, updating a service it had provided during World War II.

The Auto Club continued to develop a vision for the future of transportation in Southern California. In 1986 it released the report "Freeway Development to the Year 2000: A Proposal for Future Mobility," recommending a revival of freeway building that would add four hundred miles to the system. It also sought to modernize the existing system, citing some of the lessons learned during the smooth flow of traffic during the 1984 Olympic Games. It recommended strategies—many of which were adopted—that included increased carpooling, staggered work hours, increased on-ramp metering, and quicker response to accidents and breakdowns. Club President Henry Cheshire held a news conference to announce the plan saying Southern California's future economy depended on mobility.

Two West German athletes celebrate their arrival at the welcoming tent at LAX. All athletes first visited the tent, presented their visas and were given Olympic identification documents before being bused to their respective villages

The disco at the UCLA Olympic Village (above) as well as the one at the USC Village hosted top entertainment every night. Slaughter remembers, "They only had one week to put the villages together. It was like an army had been mobilized."

The climax of the preparations (top) was Sunday's opening ceremony. The dress rehearsal (above) was held on Thursday, and the LAOOC staff and their families were invited to attend. Slaughter remembers his feelings on opening day. "It was sheer exhaustion; every day had been like a charge of electricity . . . it was the experience of a lifetime."

kid." He now specializes in location commercial photography for magazines like *Travel and Leisure, Time, Business Week* and *Fortune.*

Slaughter's employment with the LAOOC ended in September, but his photos will live on in a two-volume report on the Games to be assembled here and forwarded to the international committee. Slaughter says he feels very fortunate to have been part of the event. "I was working with a lot of high energy people devoted to putting this on regardless. When I walked into the LAOOC's offices in Culver City, it was like someone put an electric charge into me and I stayed that way until I left there at night."

Asked if he had anything coming up in the future that's of the same magnitude as his Olympic spring and summer, Slaughter answered quickly, "Not tomorrow."

Like the first Olympiad held in Los Angeles, in 1932, the 1984 Summer Olympics presented an opportunity to showcase the most important city on the West Coast as it stood on the threshold of unprecedented expansion across the Pacific Rim. The stadium in Exposition Park that was a primary venue when the city hosted its first Olympic event was refurbished for such ceremonies as the opening and closing ceremonies and track and field events.

Income from sales of personalized license plates with the Olympic logo of five intertwined rings is one of the many licensing ventures that earned the Los Angeles Olympics the distinction of generating a profit for the first time in the game's history.

New technology and the wholesale adaptation of computers for basic office functions changed workplaces, including the Auto Club, at the end of the 1980s. The miraculous functions of the first computers purchased by the Club in the late 1950s soon became commonplace on terminals at nearly every employee's desk.

Focus on Education and Safety

Education of drivers and future motorists, always a cornerstone of the Auto Club's mission, gained renewed emphasis in the 1970s and 1980s. As had taken place for decades, the Club organized safety committees in elementary and junior high schools and instructed students in safety basics. The Auto Club continued to produce films and videotapes to instruct students in safety as pedestrians, school bus passengers, and as drivers, and it distributed millions of school safety posters. In 1970 the Auto Club estimated it had reached more than 2,650,000 youngsters since its safety programs began in the 1920s.

The public showed growing concern about the effects of drinking and driving, and in 1983 the Auto Club introduced an alcohol education curriculum designed for elementary schools to augment Auto Club lesson plans already available at the middle and senior high levels. By 1987, 48 percent of elementary and 62 percent of junior high schools had incorporated the Club's alcohol education programs into their curricula.

Safety concerns extended to car maintenance. Surveys of a random cross-section of the Auto Club's membership showed that there was a growing desire for diagnostic services. Centers were established to inspect members' automobiles, a service that evolved into "mobile" vans that took and still take close looks at cars by appointment at district offices. Classes in basic car care were also offered as well as defen-

Solar-powered vehicles, prototypes of future transportation, have been designed and tested by today's college students. The Automobile Club of Southern California sponsored the efforts of a group from California State University, Los Angeles, whose *Solar Eagle* in 1993 claimed third prize in a national race—it might have swept the field had it not suffered a massive electrical failure. It is nineteen feet long and six feet wide but stands only thirty-nine inches above the pavement; 8,500 silicon solar cells mounted on its surface have powered the car to more than 80 mph. "Solar cars draw attention to the impact engineers can have on real-world issues," said an Auto Club representative, noting that the organization has been studying the effects of fossil fuels on air quality since the 1940s.

sive driving clinics and safe boating classes. To aid car owners seeking reliable repair service, the Auto Club successfully worked for legislation to require that garages offer an estimate of repair charges before providing service.

Expanding Travel Services

Despite the high cost of gasoline, Auto Club members increasingly made use of travel services, which had begun in the 1950s to venture out of state and overseas. Expanding beyond motor adventures, the Auto Club's travel agency booked voyages by air and by cruise ships, tapping into the AAA's national reservations network. A million members made use of the services, planning 200,000 trips. More than 175,000 reservations were made at AAA-approved accommodations.

In 1970, the Auto Club introduced its TripTik system, an evolved version of the strip maps it had published since 1909. These individualized guides to destinations throughout the United States and Canada showed major segments of the journey. Announced the *Auto Club News Pictorial*:

> "The highway routing map and trip plan, expressly tailored to individual needs, is unique in the travel service field. More complete and more versatile than anything offered before, it sets high new standards for leadership."

TripTiks complemented the AAA's TourBooks, providing members with recommendations for overnight stays, restaurants, and sightseeing. The Club continued to produce maps, including a map of Native American sites and lands in the Southwest. Road maps superimposed with grids by the Auto Club came into use by fire and rescue teams throughout Southern California. Helicopter search and rescue crews used the maps, as did small planes and the FAA control towers in regional airports. Field mapping teams continually checked every road on the Auto Club's maps for changes in mileage and road conditions.

In a return to its days of charting roads and developing routes, in 1972 and 1973 Club cartographers took to the highways of Baja California, anticipating the completion of Highway 1 running from Baja California to Alaska, and to prepare maps and guidebooks. "Problems of communication and travel will gradually fade into history," the surveyors predicted, "when the new highway is completed and Baja California enters what it confidently expects will be a new era of progress and prosperity."

Although the signposting program had been discontinued in 1956, the Auto Club continued to serve on the State Traffic Control Devices Committee. Club engineers provided advice on improving sign design and placement with the goal of increasing safety and reducing confusion and frustration. This expertise came in handy in planning for the 1984 Summer Olympics. Area residents were astounded at how smoothly traffic flowed during the games. Some credit can go to pregame seminars organized by the Auto Club and UCLA that identified potential problems and developed solutions that included increased signage throughout the region. *Westways* published tips for avoiding "Olympian traffic congestion":

> "Courteous, clear-headed driving behavior can do a great deal to reduce driving stress and reduce the risk of accidents. The bottom line is this: beating Olympian traffic congestion needn't be a Herculean effort. In fact, you may find that individually and together, we can do a great deal to keep the freeways and streets moving with sportsmanlike grace."

In the 1980s the Auto Club continued to grow, largely because of its strong reputation for service to its members. Membership in Los Angeles County was augmented by significant growth in San Diego, San Bernardino, Riverside, Orange, and Ventura counties, and the Auto Club built a new processing center in Costa Mesa, which opened in 1982. Perhaps the biggest concerns the Auto Club faced in the late 1980s were rising insurance costs and uncertain local, national, and global economies. Clearly, Southern California and the Auto Club were at a crossroads. 🅰

In 1997 a spacious facility in Costa Mesa that the Automobile Club had used as a processing center was expanded to house its administrative offices. It is outfitted to accommodate the technological needs with which the membership must be served today and in the future.

6

"We're Always with You"

1990–2000

Otto the Auto, a robotic car, is visiting schools to help young children understand basic rules of automotive and pedestrian safety.

"At the Auto Club, the future of transportation in Southern California is always foremost in our minds. Keeping Californians mobile will require a commitment to preserving the investment we have already made in our transportation systems, as well as a commitment to adopting bold, innovative approaches."
—WESTWAYS, SEPTEMBER 2000

IN 1971 THE AUTO CLUB OF SOUTHERN CALIFORNIA published a four-part report in *Westways* called "Toward a Better Tomorrow" that presented its vision of the region in the year 2000. The Club's Highway Engineering Department predicted a future in which population growth could be sustained and yet mobility was still possible. They predicted a population of 21 million in Southern California (preliminary 2000 census figures total nearly 22 million). The report also predicted that Southern California would remain relatively low density. By the 1990s, some of these changes had begun to take place—in part because of the Auto Club's leadership role in making the automobile a safe, efficient, and viable means for transportation in the Southland.

By the 1990s the air was cleaner over Southern California than at any time since the 1940s. The most effective step toward arresting the air pollution that threatened to choke the region had been improvements in automotive design made by manufacturers, an approach long advocated by the Auto Club. By 1998 cars burned nearly 95 percent cleaner than their 1970 counterparts. But the number of automobiles on the road counterbalanced that good news—auto registrations had more than quadrupled since 1955. The average number of miles each car traveled increased 22 percent from 1969 to 1990. Mean travel time to work had escalated nearly 14 percent in the San

Waldo H. Burnside

Edward M. Carson

Thomas V. McKernan Jr.,
President, Chief Executive Officer

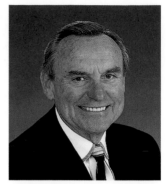

Bryon E. Allumbaugh

Susan Corrales-Diaz

Janet T. Davidson

Antonia Hernandez

Ray Martin

Donn B. Miller

Joan A. Payden

Gilbert T. Ray

Willis B. Wood, Jr.

At the end of the twentieth century Auto Club Board members, including CEO Tom McKernan, continued the efforts begun in the early 1990s to meet the challenges of the twenty-first century. Board members emphasized public affairs programs and increased the diversity of Club products and services to meet changing member needs and expectations.

Diego metropolitan area, and nearly 12 percent in the Los Angeles metropolitan area. In the same span of time, however, road capacity increased only 29 percent. Congestion on California's freeways was 65 percent higher than the national average.

Reinventing the Wheel

Air pollution and congestion were not the only challenges in the external environment. At the beginning of the 1990s, the economy of Southern California was uncertain, which in turn affected the Auto Club and its operations. One key area in need of transformation was the Interinsurance Exchange, which had been forced to raise premiums due to mounting insurance costs. After a thorough revamping of all its underwriting and claims operations, and the adoption of new technology as a means to contain operating costs, the Interinsurance Exchange started to lower rates sig-

The *Los Angeles Times*, in an article from August 1999, heralded recent management decisions that helped the Club renew its vision for a viable future in the twenty-first century.

Into Higher Gear

With aggressive new management, the Auto Club, long stuck in the slow lane, is again among the state's leading insurers. But the changes have brought some criticism too.

By LIZ PULLIAM
TIMES STAFF WRITER

Seven years ago, the Automobile Club of Southern California was on the brink of financial disaster.

Years of insurance premium hikes had driven away hundreds of thousands of the club's customers. Financial reserves were perilously low, and there was little money to invest in new facilities and technologies. At the same time, competitors were making deep inroads into the Auto Club's core businesses of emergency roadside and travel services. Layoffs and branch closures seemed inevitable; there was even talk of shuttering the club's decades-old insurance business for good.

Today, the Auto Club is once again one of the state's leading insurers, and 43% of Southern California households carry the familiar white, red and blue membership card. The not-for-profit organization has quietly grown into a financial services powerhouse that offers

Please see TURNAROUND, D15

Someone had to face the fact that times had changed, says Auto Club Chief Executive Tom McKernan, above. At left, a club technician performs a checkup on a member's vehicle.

Photos by RICK MEYER / Los Angeles Times

Lower Rates, More Policies

Lower auto insurance premiums, new services and an expansion into financial services have helped the Auto Club reach into more Southern California households.

PRICES
After years of raising auto insurance premiums, the Auto Club began cutting rates in 1993, hoping to attract more customers.

Date	Rate Change
January 1986	+10.9%
January 1987	+10.7
July 1987	+4.9
January 1988	+12.5
July 1989	+6.8
July 1993	−5.0
May 1994	−5.0
October 1996	−2.9
January 1997	−5.0
October 1997	−2.4

Source: Automobile Club of Southern California

CUSTOMERS
Thousands of consumers responded by switching their auto insurance policies to the club.
Total no. of Auto Club policies, in thousands
711,072

PENETRATION
Percentage of Southern California households that include at least one Auto Club member
43.3%

Los Angeles Times

Richard Robison, President of the Auto Club from 1987 to 1991, presided over a period of transition for the Club during the 1980s as it headed toward a decade of unprecedented success in the 1990s.

nificantly in 1993. By 1998 its financial strength exceeded the industry average.

The Auto Club made its operations more efficient and its services to members more cost effective while ensuring that the quality of its services and programs remained high. The Auto Club consolidated a number of district offices to focus assistance where there was member demand. At the end of its first century, the Club had sixty-seven offices from the Mexican border to Paso Robles, networked to a central computer. To improve the speed and quality of walk-in service, the Auto Club introduced an express service area for members with less complex needs and provided its staff with immediate computer access to all areas of Club service.

In 1997 the Auto Club relocated its administrative offices to the Processing Center it had opened in Costa Mesa in 1982. The headquarters remains in downtown Los Angeles, providing claims, travel and other services to members. The new offices' flexible floor plan, ample parking, and up-to-date networked computer systems help the organization meet the rapidly changing needs of its members and staff.

A Century of Service

During the 1990s, the Auto Club continued its legacy of service to its members. Some programs continued based on initiatives developed nearly one hundred years before,

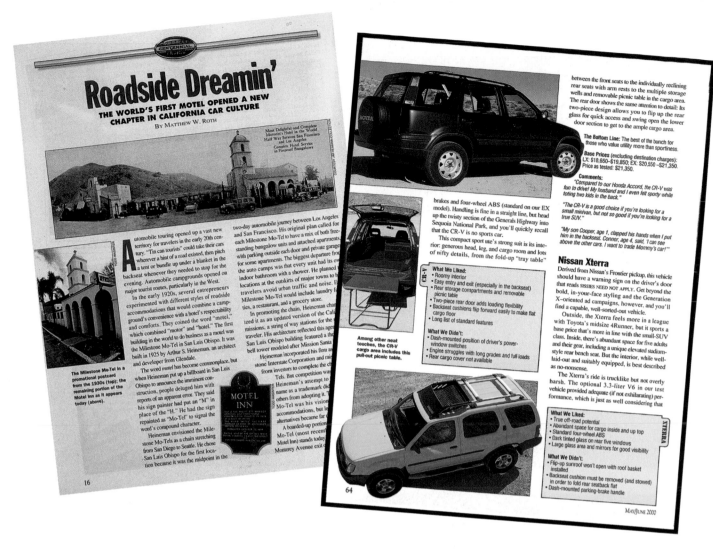

Conscious of its role as custodian of Southern California history, the Auto Club has organized its archives of some 30,000 photographs and negatives to generate exhibitions and publications that familiarize the public with its involvement in regional development. Historian Matthew W. Roth revisited "the world's first motel" and examined its role in the uniquely Californian culture of the automobile in a recent issue of the Club's signature publication. *Westways* offers practical advice to consumers based on scientific testing and evaluation: for example, which SUV offers the best features, best value for consumers in the 1990s?

number of cars on the road. Issues currently at the forefront are using new technologies and other methods to effectively manage congestion and improve mobility.

As with its promotion of California's scenic wonders from its earliest outings and runs, the Auto Club continues to focus on its members' tourism needs. Under cooperative agreements with a variety of businesses, the Auto Club offers discounts on travel and recreation throughout Southern California. More than 750,000 members participated in the "Show Your Card & Save" program, enjoying savings of up to 25 percent on car rentals, travelers' checks, hotels, and such destinations as Sea World, Universal Studios and Disneyland.

After a hiatus of many years, the Auto Club returned to its racing roots by sponsoring major Southern California motor sports events, including the NASCAR Auto Club 300 and the NHRA Hot Rod Reunion. The Club is also one of many sponsors of the Grand Prix in Long Beach. The Auto Club sponsors NHRA funny car drivers Gary Densham and Tony Pedregon who frequently promote traffic safety and vocational educational programs to junior high and high school students. The programs include "Road to the Future," which made its debut in 1999 to motivate high school students to think about their futures while introducing them to possible automotive careers.

In its tradition of being in the vanguard of technological change, the Auto Club

Its traditional services have made Southland motorists loyal Auto Club members for a century. Emergency road service has been cited as the primary reason why new and renewing members participate in the Club since this service was inaugurated in the 1920s.

developed a website that allows members to book travel, including car rental, and hotel reservations—and to search back issues of *Westways*. Members still have the choice, of course, of handling their travel arrangements in person at district offices and picking up maps and TourBooks or making arrangements by telephone, a service that began in the 1990s.

As a service to the community, the Auto Club, recognizing the pivotal place it has occupied in Southern California's development, seeks to celebrate its legacy and makes its history available to researchers, scholars, and others fascinated by the Auto Club's—and the region's—rich history. This initiative includes an exhibition program and the organization of its photographic archives and art collections, which began in 1992. The archives include some 25,000 photographs, many of them taken for *Touring Topics* and *Westways*. Many others served such prosaic purposes as documenting engineering studies. They also recorded activities such as signposting, Emergency Road Service, and transportation planning. In partnership with California museums from Ventura to Los Angeles and Palm Springs, the Club has used its archives to develop exhibits on the California desert landscape, the creation of the Pacific Coast Highway, and the depiction of the car culture in American photography.

The Auto Club has provided event support for Pasadena's annual Tournament of Roses Parade since the 1920s. Maps of the parade route and parking areas were supplied and published in local newspapers. In the 1990s the Club began sponsoring and building floats for the parade including this 1996 entry, "Animals are Awesome", which won that year's "Past President's" Trophy.

In 1996, the Auto Club expanded its horizon by assuming responsibility for AAA operations in Texas, New Mexico, and Hawaii. Members in these states can now receive benefits that mirror those that have been long available in Southern California.

The Road Ahead

What is on the road ahead for the Auto Club in the new century? Continuing service to its members is a priority. Excellence and innovation are also priorities. Looking to the future, the Auto Club supports continued development of cleaner engines for cars and alternative fuels such as electricity. It supports multiple transportation options for Southern California residents, such as light rail and smarter bus service. It is studying new transportation technologies, such as Intelligent Transportation Systems (ITS), which includes an advanced computer sensing system that would provide continuously updated guidance and control for the individual automobile, the highway, and interconnected highway systems. These electronic controls could improve the safety and carrying capacity of the roadways while reducing congestion and air pollution.

Good roads—the Auto Club's first rallying cry—remain an important concern in the coming century. In 1999 the California state legislature surveyed the state's trans-

Road races, supported by the Auto Club from 1903 to 1915 to showcase the excitement of motoring in its pioneer phase, are again featured on the roster of events in which the Club participates. The cutting edge vehicles that compete in the races highlight advances in automotive technology.

portation requirements, identifying more than $100 billion in unfunded needs. To meet these needs, the Auto Club again, as it has in the past, is shaping a transportation vision for the future. And just as it has in the past, the Auto Club will be working with community leaders and elected officials on the vision's implementation in the new millennium.

Again and again the Auto Club has made history, and based on its experience and innovative spirit, there is little doubt that it will continue to do so, changing and adapting as priorities and needs change. How far indeed the Auto Club and the region have come in one hundred years. From a handful of enthusiasts to five million people in nearly half the homes in the region, from a social club to a service organization that reaches more people in the area than any other nongovernmental organization, the Auto Club has endured in a California that barely resembles the world of 1900. Facing the future and drawing on its past, the Auto Club's staff looks forward to providing another century of service, ready to meet the challenges and opportunities on the road ahead.